INSIGHT POCKET GUIDE

BRITTANY

D1323786

Discovery
CHANNEL

APA PUBLICATIONS
Part of the Langenscheidt Publishing Group   L

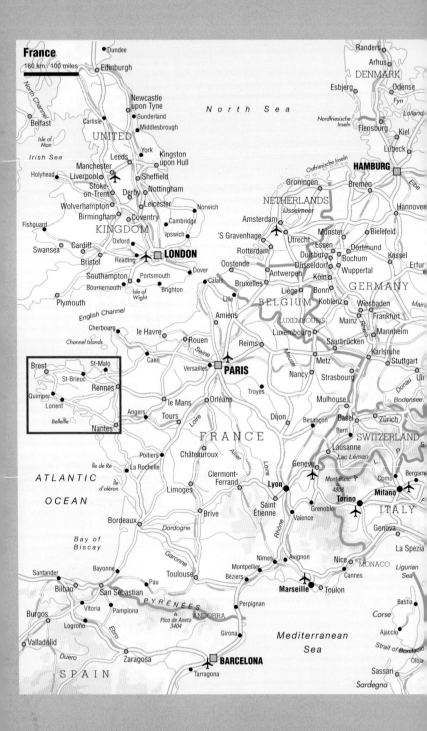

Welcome!

This guidebook combines the interests and enthusiasms of two of the world's best-known information providers: Insight Guides, who have set the standard for visual travel guides since 1970, and Discovery Channel, the world's premier source of non-fiction television programming.

In these pages, Insight Guides' expert on Brittany, travel journalist Nigel Tisdall, takes you to those parts of Brittany that are essentially Breton rather than simply Gallic. The guide opens with five full-day drives along the Emerald and Pink Granite coasts, over the heathlands of the Armorica Regional Park, through the orchards of Cornouaille, and to the forests inland. Eight options introduce Brittany's historic cities and ports, guiding you round St Malo and Dinan, Quimper and Vannes, while a further section points you to the best beaches and islands. Fleshing out the background to what you see and experience are sections on history and culture, festivals, shopping and cuisine.

Nigel Tisdall's first tour of Brittany was by bicycle. His memories of that first holiday – Dinard's classy beach with its rows of elegant striped beach tents, the wayside calvaries with their tearful but forgiving Christs, and an old man cycling in his clogs – have drawn him back countless times over the years. In this guide, it gives him great pleasure to share his love for the region with you.

History & Culture

From King Arthur and the Celts to the Duchess Anne and Gauguin, an introduction to the people that have shaped the history and culture of Brittany......................**10–17**

Day Itineraries

These five full-day itineraries take you to the highlights of Brittany

Day 1: Côte d'Emeraude: St Malo to Le Val-André begins in St Malo and heads west along the coast, calling at *Dinard*, *Fort la Latte* and *Pléhérel-Plage* or *Sables d'Or-les-Pins* **20**

Day 2: Côte de Granit Rose: Paimpol to St Michel-en-Grève explores the northernmost tip of Brittany, including the *Abbaye de Beauport*, the *Ile de Bréhat*, *Tréguier* and *Port Blanc*...**25**

Day 3: Parc Régional d'Armorique: Huelgoat to Locronan journeys through the woods and moorlands of the *Monts d'Arré* to the *Crozon Peninsula*...............**30**

Day 4: Cornouaille: Bénodet to Mur-de-Bretagne focuses on the southwest coast, a verdant region associated with artists **33**

Day 5: Morbihan: Vannes to Paimpont explores inland Brittany, beginning in *Vannes*, Brittany's medieval capital, and continuing to *Josselin*.........................**39**

Pick & Mix Itineraries

These eight suggestions are intended for visitors with more time.

1 St Malo is a guided walk through *St Malo*, with special emphasis on its splendid fortifications......................**44**

2 Cancale focuses on a small oyster-catching town east of St Malo. Includes an oyster lunch..............................**49**

3 Dinan is a bustling picturesque town overlooking the Rance valley **53**

4 Parish Closes visits three religious institutions, *St Thégonnec*, *Guimiliau* and *Lampaul-Guimiliau*.................**57**

5 Roscoff investigates the arrival and departure point for many British visitors to Brittany. Includes a visit to the Charles-Pérez Aquarium and the Tropical Gardens.........**61**

6 Quimper is devoted to the ancient capital of *Cornouaille*, which has a strong Celtic identity **63**

7 Carnac explores one of the world's great prehistoric sites comprising 2,792 standing stones..............**67**

Pages 2/3:
Dinan

8 Vannes spends the day in one of the liveliest and most attractive old towns in Brittany...**71**

Excursions

This section is devoted to other attractions, not included in the itineraries. It includes offshore islands, a round-up of the best beaches, trips by boat and recommended walks.

9 Islands tells you how to get to a few of the interesting islands off Brittany's rugged coast **76**

10 Beaches pinpoints the best of Brittany's glorious beaches..**81**

11 Sea, River and Canal Trips suggests some interesting trips that can be taken on the water.....................**84**

12 Walks caters to all grades of walkers and includes coastal paths, country trails, towpaths and forest walks **88**

Dining Experiences & Shopping
An introduction to regional specialities and tips on what to buy to take home...**95–104**

Activities & Sports
A list of *châteaux*, gardens, museums and thalassotherapy centres, followed by ideas on where to fish, ride horses, play golf, etc **105–111**

Pages 8/9: typically Breton.

Calendar of Events
A guide to festivals throughout the year **112–115**

Practical Information
All the essential background information you are likely to need for your stay, from when to visit and how to get there to business hours, accommodation, driving tips and dealing with emergencies. **116–128**

Maps
France....................................	**4**	*St Malo*...............................	**45**
Brittany....................	**18–19**	*Cancale*	**49**
Côte d'Emeraude.............	**20**	*Dinan*	**53**
Côte d'Granit Rose.........	**25**	*Parish Closes*...................	**59**
Parc Régional		*Roscoff*..............................	**61**
d'Amorique	**30**	*Quimper*.............................	**64**
Cornouaille.......................	**34**	*Carnac*	**69**
Morbihan...........................	**39**	*Vannes*...............................	**71**

Credits and Index 129–132

Land of King Arthur

Two elements etch the soul of Brittany. First there is the sea, which assaults and tatters the region on three sides, carving a jagged coastline of rocky protrusions and sandy seclusions that extends for some 750 miles (1,207km). Then there is the granite that forms its ancient core, the Armorican Massif. Today the Arrée and Noires moorlands, still described as *montagnes,* remind us of the great mountain chain that once arose here, now weathered low and drowned by a rising sea that has deeply indented the shoreline.

Modern Brittany covers an area of 27,184 sq km (10,495 sq miles), slightly larger than Wales, and it has as much in common with that country and the others of western Europe's Celtic fringe as it does with the main bulk of France. Indeed it was the Celts arriving here in the 6th century BC who gave the region its first known name – Ar-mor, land of the sea. In due course the inland areas, then covered in dense primeval forests, were christened Ar-goat, land of the wood. For centuries Brittany would remain a land deeply divided between those who farmed and those who fished, a cultural binary that is only now breaking down as we witness the emergence of a third group – those who cater to the demands of tourists.

The first Celts who settled here must have been as perplexed as we are by the enigmatic megalithic litter that has lain strewn throughout Brittany since 5,000BC. These menhirs, dolmens and cromlechs (the very words we use to describe these monuments and graves are Breton) were the work of neolithic and Early Bronze Age tribes about which we know virtually nothing – save that they left us one of the most elaborate conundrums in prehistory.

Such monuments are only one of the many mysteries that cloud early Breton history and enrich its folklore. Brittany is rightly called a land of legends: a home of King Arthur and his knights, the tempestuous background for the romance of Tristan and Iseult, a fitting location for the drowned city of Ys.

The Christian missionary

'Bataille de Brigands',
by Sébastien Vrancx

A street in Morlaix, 1830, by Jules Noël

saints who came here from Britain in the 6th century AD commandeered these myths, just as their disciples capped the pagan megaliths with crosses to proclaim the new religion. Even today the Breton heavens are well-populated with local saints, many of whom have yet to enter the official panoply but who are nevertheless frequently honoured at roadside calvaries, in stained glass, and at the Bretons' unique act of religious devotion, the *pardon*.

This rich spiritual heritage, combined with the region's natural isolation, forged a sense of Breton nationhood that has continually sought to distance itself from the rest of France. In 845 Nominoë, Brittany's first national hero, made this feeling plain when he overthrew the region's Frankish rulers and declared himself head of an independent kingdom.

It was to take another 700 years before the French monarchy finally incorporated Brittany into their disparate union of provinces. During these centuries the region became a battleground, firstly for the long-running medieval wars between the French and the English, and secondly for the feuding of its own rival nobles. Yet these times also knew peace, and by the turn of the 15th century the Duchy of Brittany was enjoying its so-called 'golden age' under Duke Jean V – a time of prosperity born of maritime trading and the production of sailcloth.

In 1488 the Duchess Anne succeeded to the Breton throne *(see panel on page 12)* and her marriage to the French King Charles VIII three years later effectively marked the end of Brittany's independence. The region now became a neglected and backward part

11

Stained glass, Dinan

The Duchess Anne

Crowned Duchess of Brittany at the age of 11, Anne (1477–1514) was the last sovereign to rule over an independent Brittany. When she was only 13 it was decided by marital engineers at the French court that Anne should marry King Charles VIII, then aged 21. It was a tempestuous courtship: Charles besieged Rennes for three months in pursuit of his claim and Anne was forced to seek the annulment of her marriage by proxy to Maximilian of Austria, heir to the Holy Roman Emperor.

They married in 1491 and this union born of politics is said to have kindled a warm love. Seven years later Charles died from an accidental blow to the head. Anne became Queen of France for a second time when she married his rapidly divorced successor, Louis XII, in 1499.

For the next fifteen years Anne was left to govern her Duchy, a swansong reign during which she secured valuable rights of independence for her subjects. When she died in 1514 at the age 37 she was universally mourned, a champion of the Breton cause whose name is now emblazoned on hotels, *crêperies* and ferry boats throughout the entire region.

of France that frequently baulked against the caprices and injustices inflicted by a quasi-colonialist central government. Riots, such as the 'Stamped Paper Revolt' of 1675 staged by armed peasants known as the Bonnets Rouges, would be provoked by new taxes on tobacco, grain or salt and always led to vicious reprisals.

Such struggles between an increasingly vociferous peasant class and an outlandish aristocracy were signs of a larger nationwide discontent that eventually boiled over in the French Revolution of 1789. At first the Bretons welcomed these events with their promise of an end to tyranny and new opportunities for self-determination. Within a year though this euphoria had turned to dismay: suddenly the Republicans had reduced Brittany to five meaningless *départements* on a map and were demanding the abolition of the Breton language. Conscription, religious persecution and the execution of the King all brought protesters on to the streets in their thousands. The arrival of 'the Terror' in 1793 provoked open support for the Royalist counter-revolutionaries known as the Chouans *(see panel, opposite)*, whose sporadic rebellions lasted until the 1830s.

Napoleon inevitably left his mark on Brittany, most clearly in the grid of streets he built in Pontivy, which for a brief period was known as Napoléonville. Under his instigation, straight roads were built through the province and the port of Lorient developed as a naval base. He also ordered the construction of the Nantes-Brest Canal, a response

The Chouans

In Brittany the euphoria inspired by the French Revolution of 1789 soon turned to disillusionment as the Bretons found their hopes for self-determination were not to be realised. By 1793 a resistance movement, the *Association Bretonne,* had been formed with the aim of recovering these former rights. When the reign of terror reverberating around France reached Brittany the atrocities committed in its hunt for counter-revolutionaries only served to win new support for their cause. One of the most barbaric incidents occurred in Nantes in October 1793 when the Convention's Deputy, Jean-Baptiste Carrier, chose to clear his over-stocked jails by loading prisoners into barges which were then towed out into the Loire and sunk.

Better known by their nickname of the *Chouans* (after the cry of the screech-owl used as an identifying signal), the members of the Association were led by a 22-year-old farmer's son, Georges Cadoudal. His forces soon became linked with the wider Royalist cause and in 1795 an attempt was made by foreign exiles to land an invasion force on the Quiberon peninsula with support from the British navy. It ended in disaster when the combined Royalist and Chouan armies, whose numbers were considerably less than the 100,000 troops envisaged, marched into a trap laid by the Revolutionary General Louis-Lazare Hoche.

The debâcle ended with some 900 prisoners being taken. Few were pardoned and the defeat marked the virtual end of the Chouans, though not of their cause or Cadoudal. In 1799 he organised new guerrilla forces to fight for Breton liberty but these were soon flushed out. Cadoudal escaped to England, returning in 1804 to launch a bizarre attempt to kidnap Napoleon. Romantically known as 'the last Chouan' he was captured and executed the same year, his body unceremoniously given to anatomy students for dismemberment.

French troops in Tréguier, 1870

Quimper, Brittany's most Celtic city

to the disruption of coastal communication between these ports caused by the English navy. The late 19th century also saw the gradual advance of the railway into Brittany, a *cheval noir* that the peasants would walk miles to see.

When Gauguin arrived in Pont-Aven in 1886 much of Brittany was still devout, conservative, parochial and superstitious. Outwardly it conformed to our severe and idyllic image of Brittany as a hardy land of box-beds and wooden *sabots* (clogs), of threshing-songs and widows waiting on the cliffs for the return of the fishing boats. *Pardons* were still well attended, the men dressed in their embroidered waistcoats, the women in their elaborate lace head-dresses known as *coiffes*. But it was also a time of insidious social change, principally in the larger cities and ports to which the rural young would drift, many often choosing to better their lot by emigration. Breton culture was also being suppressed, with humiliating measures taken to stamp out its language, such as forcing schoolchildren who spoke Breton to wear a heavy *sabot* around their necks.

These changing horizons were shattered by two world wars. It is said that in World War I Brittany suffered more deaths per capita than any other part of France. In World War II the German Occupation provoked a militant nationalist resistance movement that came to the fore in the weeks preceding D-Day.

The post-war period opened with many of Brittany's cities and ports bombed to the ground. Migrants flooded to other parts of France or abroad, and those that eventually returned came with new perceptions. Soon traditional Breton clothing and furniture were being rejected in favour of their cheaper modern equivalents. In due course the Bretons would sell their decorated box-beds and bench-chests to the early tourists, the 'Kodakers' from Paris who enjoyed that previously unheard of luxury, the paid holiday.

The 1960s saw the start of an economic renaissance in Brittany which continues today. The principal catalyst was a young Breton farmer, Alexis Gourvennec, who led a series of protests now known as 'The Artichoke War'. These demonstrations, yet another Breton rebellion against negligent overseers, brought an end to the archaic marketing system that had controlled the sale of agricultural produce in Brittany for centuries. Farmers' co-operatives were established throughout the region, which became the focus of a unified clamour for a series of changes. One demand was for a deep-water port at Roscoff so that Breton produce could be exported to the UK, a move that led to the creation of Brittany Ferries in 1973 and which has in turn transformed the nature of tourism in the region.

Today Brittany is one of the more prosperous regions of France, specialising in hi-tech goods and agriculture. It is still dogged by central controls, though, and the removal of the Loire-Atlantique *département* from the region in 1972, which included its former capital Nantes (and the Muscadet vineyards), still rankles. The tiny Breton Liberation Front still argues for independence from France, but most Bretons would settle for greater cultural autonomy. Economic progress, including the rise in tourism, has inspired a new cultural confidence. Today there is a growing respect for the Breton language and a surging Celtic pride that actively fosters Brittany's ancient links with its Celtic brethren. Brittany no longer sees itself as a part of France but – with a forethought typical of a region that has always sought to control its own destiny – as a part of Europe.

The Breton Language

The roots of the Breton language are Celtic, and visitors familiar with Welsh, Gaelic or Cornish will immediately notice the similarity.

Place-names will probably provide your first encounter with Breton vocabulary; these are often a combination of natural elements – stone *(men)*, sea *(mor)*, mountain *(menz)* or wind *(avel)* – and function, for example as a port *(pors)*, village *(ker)*, parish *(plou)* or holy place *(loc)*. Thus Huelgoat means 'high wood', and Plouhinec 'place of gorse', while other settlements may be named after local saints such as Guimilau (the town of St Miliau).

Today there are around 500,000 Bretons who still speak their native tongue, most of them over 40 years old and living in western Brittany. The International Committee for the Defense of the Breton Language strives to prevent Breton from dying out. The signs are encouraging, with the creation of small but thriving Breton-language TV and radio stations and publications. The Breton language is taught in many schools, and is the language of instruction for around 2 percent of school children. The Committee hopes that this will rise to 5 or 10 percent by 2010: young speakers using the Breton language daily in their homes and communities are the key to its survival.

Historical Highlights

450,000BC Artefacts found at St Columban, the oldest prehistoric site in Brittany, reveal the presence of nomadic tribes in the region during palaeolithic times.

5,000 Start of the megalith-building period. During the next 3,000 years thousands of stone monuments are erected throughout Brittany by unknown neolithic and Early Bronze Age settlers.

6th century Celts from Central Europe spread north through Gaul. They give the region its first known name: Armor, land of the sea.

AD56 Caesar's armies defeat the most powerful tribe in Armorica, the Veneti. The Romans build towns and roads that form the basis of many present-day settlements such as Nantes, Rennes and Vannes.

5th century The Romans withdraw their legions. As the Anglo-Saxons invade England many native Celts flee across the Channel. Some establish new colonies in Armorica which they rename Little Britain —hence the region's modern name.

6th century Birth of Breton culture. Celtic mysticism is tempered by the teachings of Christian missionary saints like Malo, Brioc and Pol-de-Léon.

799 Charlemagne, King of the Franks, conquers Brittany. The region becomes part of an empire covering most of western Europe.

826 Charlemagne's son, Louis the Pious, creates the duchy of Brittany. Its first Duke, Nominoë, rebels against Frankish rule to win independence in 845. It is shortlived but marks the establishment of the region's boundaries and the start of its struggle for self-determination.

919 The Normans overrun Brittany but are expelled 20 years later by the last Breton king, Alain Barbe-Torte. On his death in 952 feuding breaks out between rival nobles.

1066 The Norman Conquest of Britain: from now on the history of Brittany will be forever entangled with the tortured affairs of England and France.

1337 Start of the Hundred Years War between England and France. In Brittany both sides contest the 'War of Succession'.

1341–64 Bertrand du Guesclin rises to fame as a military commander.

1351 'Battle of the Thirty' takes place near Ploërmel.

1364 The Dukes of Montfort restore order to the region, skilfully pursuing a course of neutrality between rival factions. A century of renewed prosperity and cultural energy ensues as maritime trade flourishes. Many churches built.

1491 Anne of Brittany marries Charles VIII, King of France. Brittany remains an independent duchy but is now effectively a part of France.

1532 The permanent union of Brittany and France is ratified by the Vannes parliament.

1534 Jacques Cartier, born in Rothéneuf, discovers the mouth of the St Lawrence river.

16th–17th century Sporadic periods of lawlessness and rebellion result from the half-hearted efforts of the French monarchy to govern Brittany. The most serious of these is the revolt of the Bonnets Rouges (1675), a widespread protest by peasants against punitive taxes which is ruthlessly suppressed by the army.

As a result, the Breton parliament is suspended for 15 years. Construction of the parish closes in Finistère.

1722 Fire destroys most of the Breton capital, Rennes.

1789 The French Revolution is welcomed by the Bretons. However the advent of conscription, religious persecution and the Terror, along with the unpopular execution of the King and the banning of the Breton language, brings disillusionment.

1795 The Royalist Chouans become the focus of a doomed attempt to launch a counter-revolution with the help of exiled and foreign forces.

1836 Opening of the Nantes-Brest canal.

1886–95 Gauguin and other artists of the 'Pont-Aven' school working in Cornouaille.

1911 The Breton separatist party, Strollad Broadel Breisz, is founded.

1914–18 World War I exacts a heavy death toll.

1939–45 World War II. The entire male population of the Ile de Sein are amongst the first to answer General de Gaulle's call to join him in exile in England. The Breton Resistance smuggles hundreds of Allied airmen across the Channel. Many Breton cities are badly damaged.

1960 The 'Artichoke War' becomes the focus for a restructuring of the way Brittany's agricultural produce is marketed. It marks the start of an economic renaissance.

1972 A change of official boundaries removes the *département* of Loire-Atlantique from Brittany.

1977 Diwan, the first Breton language schools network, is established.

1989 High-speed TGV rail link opens between Paris and Brest.

1994 Opening of the Channel Tunnel linking France and England.

1999 A woman is killed by a bomb planted by the armed wing of the Breton separatist movement. The Maltese-registered oil tanker *Erika* sinks in storms, polluting much of Southern Brittany's coastline.

2000 TV-Breizh, the first Breton-language TV station, is launched in September.

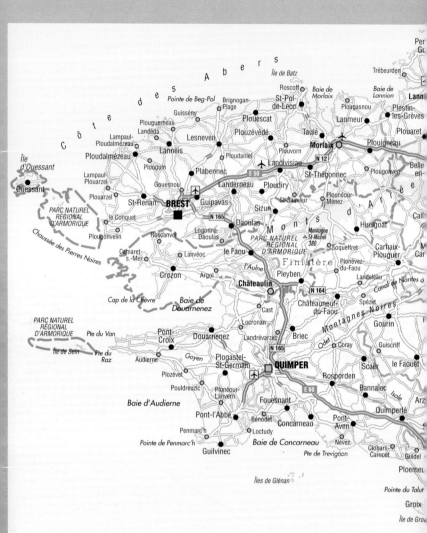

Brittany

30 km / 20 miles

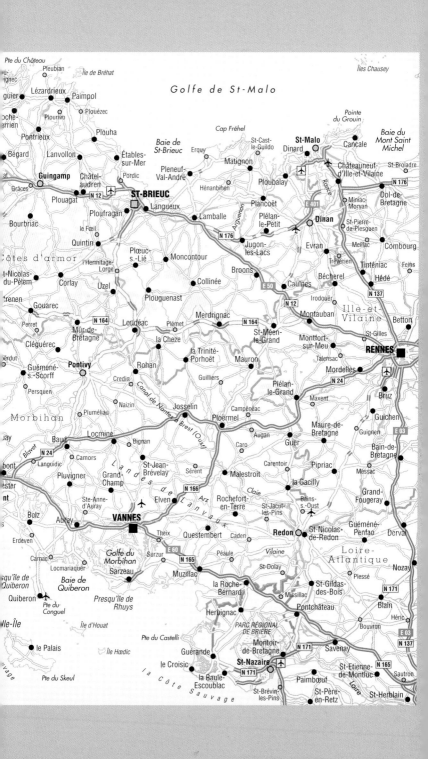

Our guide opens with five touring itineraries that will introduce you to the best of Brittany, from its dramatic coasts to the gently wooded interior. Eight optional tours then guide you round the region's historic cities and ports, and four further excursions take you to the best of Brittany's beaches and islands.

Côte d'Emeraude: St Malo to Le Val-André

Brittany's northern shoreline is a rollercoaster of rocky headlands and wide sandy beaches that grow increasingly dramatic the further you venture west. The Emerald Coast, which stretches from the Pointe du Grouin near Cancale *(see page 49)* west to Le Val-André, offers a picturesque introduction to such charms – a gentle succession of traditional resorts and quiet coves.

This itinerary begins in St Malo *(see page 44)* and idles westwards along the coast: if you prefer a more demanding day you can easily extend your route to include a morning walk round the medieval town centre of Dinan *(see page 53)*.

Leave St Malo via St Servan (D168) and cross the **Barrage de la Rance** towards Dinard. The road runs along the top of this

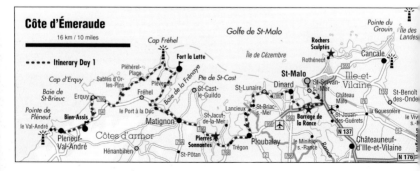

Dinard

great dam, built in 1966 and the first in the world to use tidal power to generate electricity. To your right you will see the triple towers of the **Tour Solidor**, built in 1382 as part of the Dukes of Montfort's efforts to oversee the unruly Malouins; it is now a fascinating museum dedicated to seafaring around Cape Horn. Its present shape dates from 1890 *(see page 47)*.

Soon after you cross the Rance turn right on to the D114 for La Vicomté, a quiet road that leads into **Dinard**. Park near the Tourist Office (tel: 02 99 46 94 12) in Boulevard Féart near the seafront. Deservedly titled 'Queen of the Emerald Coast', Dinard still has aristocratic airs bequeathed to it from the days when Victorian bathing carriages lined its Grand Plage.

Blessed with three beaches, it was 'discovered' in the 1850s after an American millionaire called Coppinger built a mansion here and inspired a rush of villa-building around St-Énogat. Today Dinard strives to remain stylish, a host to international film festivals and celebrity concerts, its beaches graced by rows of striped beach tents and groups of straw-hatted *boule* players.

The Emerald Coast

Hôtel La Vallée

For a taste of Dinard's charms walk east from the Tourist Office, down rue de Leavasseur, turning right onto Avenue George V to **Le Grand Hôtel**, built in 1859 with fine views across the Rance to St Malo. It has a relaxing bar, ideal for a late-morning coffee or pre-lunch aperitif. From here you can cross the road and descend some steps to the **Yacht Club**, on the Promenade du Clair de Lune. This walk follows the water's edge round to a small quay where the **Hôtel La Vallée** offers a restful place for an alfresco lunch. Menus here range from the simple to the gourmet — settle for an exquisite bowl of *moules marinières* or get to work on a monster *plateau de fruits de mer*.

From here you can continue around the shore to the **Pointe du Moulinet** where a viewing-table maps out the panorama ahead of you. The most noticeable sights are St Malo and the neighbouring island of Grand Bé, and further west Cézembre. The path then curls round the cliffs to the magnificent **Grand Plage**, also known as Plage de l'Écluse, its seafront dominated by the elderly Casino (1911) and the modern Olympic swimming pool (1967).

Leave Dinard along the D786 towards **St Briac-sur-Mer**, home to one of the oldest golf courses in France (Golf Dinard; *see page 111*). Here the bridge across the Frémur marks the traditional boundary between the *départements* of Ille-et-Vilaine and Côtes d'Armor — in 1990 the latter changed its name from Côtes du Nord after a long campaign to avoid confusion with the eastern *département* Nord.

Continue south past the rocket-ship spire of **Lancieux's church**, skirting **Ploubalay** and winding on through **Matignon**. Such villages sport all the characteristic hallmarks of modern Brittany — bullied by traffic, their granite walls are bedecked with *crêperie* signs and chalked blackboards advertising freshly caught mussels and oysters.

Fort la Latte

Continue along the southern shore of the vast rectangular Baie de la Frênaye, taking the first right after the bridge on to a minor road that runs alongside the estuary before climbing inland into woods to join the D16A – follow the signs (a series of right turns) to La Motte and then Fort la Latte.

Built on top of a rocky spur, **Fort la Latte** is a story-book castle that seems far too picturesque to have seen battle (Apr–Sep: 10am–12.30pm and 2.30–6.30pm; Oct–Mar: Saturday and Sunday and holidays 2.30–5.30pm and by appointment; call the tourist office at Fréhel, tel: 96 41 53 81). Set in a park, it's a 10-minute from the entrance gates to its fortified drawbridges. Constructed in the 13th century by the Goyon-Matignon family, the castle was remodelled in the 17th by the great military architect Vauban.

Its steep walls have played host to a curious parade of historical characters including, in 1715, James Stuart (The Old Pretender) during his ill-fated bid for the English throne; English spies captured

Pléhérel-Plage

after the French Revolution; a troop of White Russians billeted here in the World War II; and, in 1957, the cast of a Hollywood epic starring Kirk Douglas and Tony Curtis, *The Vikings*. Today only video cameras shoot from its ramparts and the rusty cannon on its outposts lie rotting in the sea-spray, but the fort still impresses: if you climb up to the watchtower you'll find the commanding views of the north coast are just as they were centuries ago.

Leave Fort la Latte and follow the signs west to **Cap Fréhel** (D16), one of the most panoramic (and popular) headlands in northern Brittany, and excellent for invigorating coastal walks. The tall silhouette of its lighthouse, easily visible from Fort la Latte, dominates the cliffs which rise sheer from the sea to nearly 250ft (75m), the highest part of the Emerald Coast.

After the windblown moorland of Cap Fréhel the road (D34A) leads west to a softer landscape of heather and pines. Here the Breton coast performs one of its enchanting cabarets as every beach you pass appears more magical and inviting than the last. Be sure to stop for a walk along the shore, perhaps at **Pléhérel-Plage** or at the aptly named resort of **Sables d'Or-les-Pins**.

If you're camping, the sites along this stretch of the coast are idyllic and you should stop soon. Further along the coast (D786) more spectacular beaches greet you – **Erquy** has an enormous stretch of pale golden sand, as does **Le Val-André** further west. Both of these resorts have modest hotels ideal for passing travellers who like a long evening stroll on the sands and a quiet night's rest. Strung out along the seafront, Le Val-André has a beguiling period feel, part-Victorian, part-1930s. For an enjoyable meal to crown your day, the **Hôtel-Restaurant de la Mer** here offers home-cooking based on local seafood (63 Rue A Charner, tel: 02 96 72 20 44).

Cap Fréhel lighthouse

Côte de Granit Rose: Paimpol to St Michel-en-Grève

Stretching unevenly from Paimpol to Trébeurden, the Pink Granite Coast is an undulating landscape of wide beaches and low cliffs fringed with reefs and outlying rocks. Strewn with enormous boulders, many of which have been eroded into curious shapes, it has a surreal aspect most obvious when the evening sun ignites the pink granitic rocks that blush their deepest between Trégastel and Trébeurden.

Granite boulder, Trégastel

While most of this itinerary can be covered in a day it is best spread over two, something essential if you plan to visit the Ile de Bréhat or linger on the beach for any length of time. Tréguier or Port Blanc might be convenient places to break your journey. As in many parts of northern Brittany the coast here is graced by a multitude of quiet coves and splendid beaches that offer a relaxed alternative to the busy resorts, so be sure to have the ingredients for an impromptu picnic on board.

The itinerary begins at the **Pointe de Bilfot**, from which there is a fine panorama of the Bay of Paimpol. It can be easily reached if you take the D77 east from Plouézec, 4km (6½ miles) south of Paimpol, first following the signs for Port Lazo, then Pointe de Bilfot, where there is a viewing-table. From here the views extend northwest to the Ile de Bréhat and east to Cap Fréhel, while below an aquamarine sea relentlessly pummels the rocks. In this windswept corner of Brittany the sea has determined life for many Bretons for, from the 1850s up until the turn of the 20th century, huge

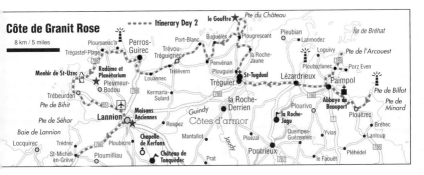

Tréguier cathedral

fishing fleets would sail out from Paimpol to catch cod off Iceland, deep-sea voyages of great hardship and tragedy that were recorded in Pierre Loti's famous novel *Pêcheur d'Islande* (1886).

Return to Plouézec and turn right along the D786 towards Paimpol. Soon you will pass the attractive Gothic ruins of the **Abbaye de Beauport**, founded in 1202 (open mid-Jun–mid-Sep daily 10am–7pm; otherwise 10am–noon and 2–5pm). Continue on the D786 towards Paimpol, a pleasant harbour town with seafood restaurants lining the seafront, including L'Islandais, which serves a good-value lunch. Take the D789 signposted north to Ploubazlanec, and turn right here down a minor road to Porz-Even. This is a quiet fishing village, its low granite houses pleasantly devoid of the gaudy trappings of seasonal tourism.

Return to Ploubazlanec and turn right along the D789 to Pointe de l'Arcouest. This is the embarkation point for the crossing to **Ile**

de Bréhat, your best chance to enjoy some sea air and a walk round one of the mildest of Brittany's many islands *(see page 76)*.

From Pointe de l'Arcouest it is simplest to return to Paimpol and and take the D786 to Tréguier. As you head west through a patchwork of cabbage fields you'll notice how the landscape is gaining a more Breton aspect: junctions are adorned with roadside calvaries, street-names are given in French and Breton, Celtic place-names become more common – often prefixed by *ker* (house or village), *plou* (parish) or *lann* (heath). The churches change too, now capped by graceful lantern towers with needle points that pierce the skyline.

Soon the silhouette of Tréguier's cathedral appears on the horizon, the principal city along the Côte de Granit Rose. **Tréguier** sits on a hill overlooking the confluence of the Jaudy and Guindy rivers – after crossing the bridge stay with the river till you reach the place Général de Gaulle (look for the Hôtel L'Estuaire), where you turn left and climb up to the place du Martray. This square is the heart of the town, dominated by the **Cathédrale de St Tugdual**. Opposite, in a typically French juxtaposition, a parade of *pâtisseries* and *salons de thé* enable visitors to combine spiritual edification with bodily fortification.

Tomb of St Yves, Tréguier cathedral

The cathedral is a masterly example of how Breton architects and stonemasons managed to make an unyielding stone like granite sing. It has three towers – the Romanesque 'Hastings' tower; an incomplete Gothic tower above the transept; and an 18th-century spire, decoratively aerated with holes to prevent the wind from destroying it.

Although dedicated to one of Brittany's 'founder-saints' St Tugdual, a Welsh monk who founded a bishopric here in the 6th century, the cathedral is also a shrine to a more recent, locally born saint, **St Yves**. As soon as you enter the porch look right and you will see a carved wooden image of him, traditionally depicted standing between a rich and a poor man.

Born in 1253, St Yves practised as a lawyer and has become the legal profession's patron saint; across the aisle, his tomb – destroyed in the lawless days of the French Revolution – is a 19th-century

copy of a monument erected in his honour by Duke Jean V, who chose to be buried alongside him.

If you like pottering along minor roads take the D8 north from Tréguier to Plouguiel and turn right down a narrow road signposted to La Roche Jaune. This marks the start of the '**Circuit de la Côte Ajoncs**', an hour-long scenic route that weaves in and around the coast — expect to see a lot of cabbages and artichokes and don't be surprised if the road signs suddenly dry up. They soon re-appear and will lead you out via Plougrescant to the **Pointe du Château** where the departing tide leaves vast swathes of glistening mud and seaweed-fringed rocks. Along here fig trees testify to the mild climate of this shore (ajoncs = gorse), and the boulders have a genuinely pinky hue, deserving the name Côte de Granit Rose.

The 'Circuit' eventually leads you through Buguélès to **Port Blanc**, which can be reached more directly from Tréguier by the D70/74. Port Blanc still has a quiet, away-from-it-all charm with its tiny, photogenic chapel perched on a rock that is surrounded by water at high tide. Here **Le Grand Hôtel** has a restaurant serving good Breton food. Alternatively, further west along the D113 there is a temptingly large pale sand beach at Trévou-Tréguignec.

From here you can take the D38 to Trélévern where a minor road (sign-posted to Perros-Guirec) leads you to Louannec. Take the D6 that drops down through chestnut woods to Perros-Guirec, where you should keep to the shore-side road (boulevard de la Mer) which skirts the port and climbs up to a good viewpoint overlooking the **Plage de Trestrignel**. You are now back in the candy-floss world of the seaside holiday — Perros-Guirec is one of the most popular resorts along this stretch of coast and its liveliest beach is the Plage de Trestraou. Your best escape route is the D788, which is known as the Corniche Bretonne, a grand title

Port Blanc

Breton fishing boat

for what is a rather average coastal road linking the resorts of Trégastel-Plage and Trébeurden.

The main attractions here are the seaside and the famous pink granite rocks. For pink granite you need look no further than the buildings around you, many of which are faced with this glistening stone, as is the bridge you cross at Ploumanach. For the more dramatic rocks that time has eroded into fascinating anthropomorphic shapes turn right by the church in Trégastel and head down to the **Plage du Coz-Porz**. There are more at **Grève Blanche**. These beaches, with their giant boulders and rock pools, should keep the kids amused for hours.

Just past Trébeurden the Pointe de Bihit (turn right off the D788) offers the chance of a view back along this coast and west towards Roscoff. From here a minor coastal road leads you back up to the D65 – continue on through Lannion and out on the D786, signposted to Morlaix. Your destination is **St Michel-en-Grève**, one of the most magnificent beaches in Brittany. Its bay cradles a 5-km (3-mile) runway of pale white sand, packed so hard it is sometimes used as a horse track for the Lannion races. If the tide's out it's an exhilarating walk of about 1.5km (1 mile) to find the sea.

Day 3

Parc Régional d'Armorique: Huelgoat to Locronan

This itinerary takes you through the best of the Parc Régional d'Armorique, a gentle descent from the woods and moorlands of the Monts d'Arrée to the windswept cliffs of the Presqu'île de Crozon. It's a long but easy drive – be sure to get to Camaret by 1pm if you want lunch.

The route begins in **Huelgoat**, a popular inland centre for walking and hiking in the surrounding hills and forests *(see page 90)*. Dotted around the Parc there are also 12 well thought-out specialist museums that provide an engaging introduction to life in Finistère past and present *(see page 106)*.

Leave Huelgoat on the D14 in the direction of Loqueffret. The road skirts the southern edge of the **Monts d'Arrée**, a ridge of flat

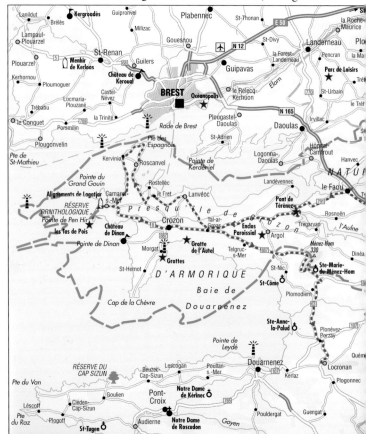

granite moorland that can only just be called mountains today – their most accessible high point is the nearby **Roc Trévezel** (384m/1,260ft), from which there are sweeping views of the surrounding countryside. About 7km (4 miles) from Huelgoat you'll find the square-towered **Chapelle St Herbot**, a lovingly tended village church with a small lichen-blotched calvary.

St Herbot is the patron saint of horned cattle and at the annual *pardon* (religious festival) held every May farmers would bring their cattle here and solemnly conduct them around the chapel. In time this became impractical so today tufts of hair from their tails are left as an offering on the two tables at the base of the chancel.

Continue on through Loqueffret to Croas-Ahars where you must turn right for **Brasparts** (D21). The village has a 16th-century parish close and calvary. As you carry on look out on your right for the skeletal ruin of **Quimerch church**, abandoned in the 1870s because it was too far from the centre of its parish. Further on you pass through the village of Ty-Jopic where you take the D770 to Le Faou.

From Le Faou take the

Parc Naturel Régional d'Armorique

16 km / 10 miles

Pointe de Pen Hir

D791 corniche road west for the Crozon Peninsula. Soon the sea appears to your right and at Pont de Térénez you cross the Aulne estuary. Now you are on the cross-shaped **Crozon Peninsula**, renowned for its wild and windy coastline but still blessed by a climate mild enough to line the road with farms selling honey, pears and cider. The road rides the spine of this *presqu'île* (peninsula) with views across to the sea.

At Tal-ar-Groas turn right (D63) for Lanvéoc and then turn left here (D55) for Le Fret. Continue past the nuclear submarine base at Ile Longue to Roscanvel (D355) and the **Pointe des Espagnols**. From this bleak point there are good views across the bay to Brest: the Pointe gets its name from an incident in 1594 during the Breton Wars of Religion when 400 Spaniards occupied the headland – they were only dislodged after a six-week struggle by 4,000 French and English troops. All along this coast you will find the ruins of forts built to defend the peninsula, many of them the work of Vauban.

Continue round the coast on the D355 to **Camaret**, a quiet fishing port with some excellent quayside fish restaurants. One of the best is on the first floor of the **Hôtel de France** (Quai G Toudouze, tel: 02 98 27 93 06). This is the place to splash out on a platter of *fruits de mer* or to try some *homard à l'Armoricaine* (lobster thermidor). Alternatively, try the Hôtel du Styval on Quai du Styval, tel: 02 98 27 92 74). Both restaurants overlook the port with its red brick fort built by Vauban in the 1690s, part of which houses La Maison du Patrimoine (open daily mid-Jun–mid-Sep 2–7pm, low season Fri–Mon only), which charts the port's long fishing history. In 1801, the American inventor Robert Fulton conducted trials of one of the world's earliest submarines in the harbour here.

The best place to walk off your lunch is the **Pointe de Pen Hir**, a short distance west on the D8. This is a bizarre cliff-top land's end, often packed with visitors who come to stare at the sea-buffeted rocks known as the **Tas de Pois** (Pile of Peas).

From here you can take the D8 back to Crozon, past some lovely sandy beaches, continuing east in the direction of Châteaulin (D887). As you rejoin the mainland the landscape returns to wild moorland.

Look for a turn off to your left for the **Ménez-Hom**, one of Brittany's highest points (330m/1,082ft). The windswept peak is essential viewing.

Return to the D887 where you will soon pass the pretty **Chapelle de Ste-Marie-du-Ménez-Hom**. Turn right here on to the

Pointe de Penhir, Resistance Monum•

D47, signposted to Quimper, and continue on the D63 through Plomodiern and Plonévez-Porzay to the postcard-perfect town of **Locronan.**

Locronan's Renaissance houses were built when the town was the centre of a canvas-making industry that supplied sailcloth to the French and Spanish navies. In the late 17th-century Louis XIV abolished the Breton monopoly on linen and the resulting decline in Locronan's fortunes helped preserve its harmonious ensemble of granite buildings around the cobbled square. Roman Polanski filmed *Tess* here.

Locronan, Chapel of Our Lady of Good News

Around 7pm there is a magical hour when the town falls quiet – this is the time to wander its mossy streets. Be sure to venture down rue Moal where there is the **Chapel of Our Lady of Good News**, its simple stonework reflected in a 17th-century fountain. Place du 10 mars 1962, accessible from a path leading up from the main car park, is the starting point for an 8-km (5-mile) circular walk around the town.

If you plan to stay overnight here, the **Hôtel du Prieuré** (tel: 02 98 91 70 89), a two-star Logis, is good value; for dinner try the **Fer à Cheval** (place de l'Église, tel: 02 98 91 70 74).

DAY ④

Cornouaille: Bénodet to Mûr-de-Bretagne

The southwest coast of Brittany, a benign landscape of gentle hills and wooded estuaries, is known as Cornouaille, named by the Celts who fled here from Cornwall in the 6th century BC.

This itinerary meanders along the verdant shore, passing through the villages and countryside that inspired painters like Gauguin and Corot, then heading inland to the dark forests of the Argoat.

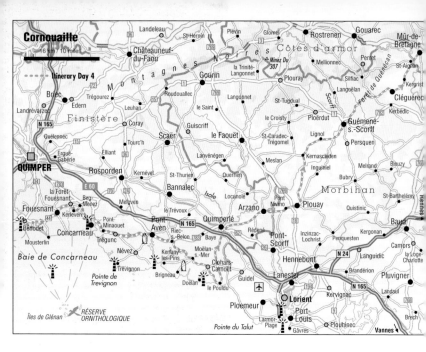

It is best taken over two days, particularly if you plan to go walking – the oak woods around Pont-Aven or the larger Forêt de Quénécan is ideal for this. Quimperlé or Le Pouldu are quiet and convenient places to break your journey. Another alternative is to carry straight on from Le Pouldu to the megaliths and beaches of Carnac *(see page 67)*.

The itinerary begins in **Bénodet**, a classic sand 'n' mud resort where every summer the roads turn to a thick jam of GB number-plates. Its position at the mouth of the Odet estuary is a winning formula where holidaymakers can happily combine messing about on the river with seaside indolence. If you're arriving from Quimper (D34) take the avenue de l'Odet from the town centre and look for a pull-off (avenue de Kercréven) where there is a good view of the Odet and Bénodet's **Port de Plaisance**. From here you can continue round along the Corniche de l'Estuaire and the Corniche de la Mer as Bénodet's long stretch of sheltered beach unrolls beside you. The road leads out to the **Pointe de Bénodet** where there are far-reaching views of the coast and yet more sandy beaches to the east. From here the road (Route du Poulinc) curls inland to join the D44, where you turn right for Fouesnant.

Continue on to La Forêt-Fouesnant, where you turn right towards Port-la-Fouesnant (ignoring the signs saying 'Concarneau par la côte', which don't take you very close to the coast). This route takes you down some delightful lanes lined with chestnut woods and cider orchards, past the fine beach of Kerleven to Beg-Menez, where you turn right down a steep hill towards Concarneau.

Concarneau is one of the biggest fishing ports in France out of which fleets sail as far as West Africa to catch tuna fish. Its principal

attraction is the well-preserved 14th-century **Ville Close** built on an island in the centre of the harbour. As you enter the port keep to the water's edge – you will pass a small chapel on the Quai de la Croix before arriving at the Quai Pénéroff. Here you can park and walk across the small bridge leading to the old town. Inside you will find a quaint tourist-trap grinning with flower-bedecked souvenir shops and restaurants. It is a place to amble through, perhaps pausing for a *crêpe* or *plat du jour*. There is a short rampart walk you can do starting just beside the entrance and a little further on is the comprehensive **Musée de la Pêche** with rooms devoted to the extraction of whales, tuna, herring and sardines from the sea (Jul and Aug daily 9.30am–8pm; rest of the year 10am–noon and 2–6pm).

Leave Concarneau on the D783, signposted to Quimperlé. The road weaves through Trégunc to **Pont-Aven**: when you arrive don't cross the bridge but continue straight on to park by the port. From here you can walk across a small footbridge, past one of Pont-Aven's many old water-mills, and back along the rue Auguste Brizeux to the town centre.

You may find this once quiet village where Gauguin and other artists came to paint in the 1880s merely an over-commercialised attempt to cash in on their achievements: the town has some 40 art galleries bathing in the masters' after-glow. And if you're hoping

Concarneau harbour

The tourist brochures would have you believe that Paul Gauguin (1848–1903) and his fellow bohemians came to Pont-Aven for the beautiful landscape and excellent *crêpes*. In fact, they came here because they were poor and Brittany was cheap. By the time Gauguin arrived in 1886 there was already an established artists' colony in Pont-Aven, part of a regular summer exodus from the Paris studios. Gauguin soon fell out of step with these Salon painters whose slick, photograph-like depictions of Breton life he detested. His objectives were more emotional: 'I love Brittany' he declared, 'I find there the savage, the primitive. When my clogs resound on this granite soil I hear the dull, matt, powerful tone that I'm after in my painting.'

The arrival of Émile Bernard in Pont-Aven in 1888 proved catalytic. Bernard re-awakened Gauguin to the piety and religious devotion of the Breton people which became a common subject for their work. They painted in a deliberately crude, almost caricatural manner using brilliant colours and fluid dark outlines around their subjects that became known as Synthesism. Gauguin's *La Lutte de Jacob avec l'Ange,* inspired by the local *pardon* at Pont-Aven, is one of the best-known examples of this style.

The following year Gauguin left the crowds of Pont-Aven for the peace of Le Pouldu, another step in a life-long process of rejection that would eventually lead him to the South Seas. At Le Pouldu, Synthesist ideas were advanced further by artists like Sérusier, Laval, de Haan and Filiger. Their work was always primarily an exploration of abstract problems – how line, colour and rhythm could be used to express mood, emotion and imagination – with the Breton landscape and its people providing a launch-pad for their investigations. Today Gauguin is credited as a major figure in the liberation of art from obedience to nature, but the work of the Pont-Aven school should be seen as more than an adjunct to his achievement.

'Bretonne de Profil' (1892), by Cuno Aimet

It provides a striking record of a Brittany that has all but vanished, a severe and superstitious land of starched *coiffés* and *pardons* where life was guided by the seasons and occasionally brightened by dancing, wrestling and regattas.

Trémalo chapel

to see plenty of Gauguin's work, you'll be disappointed. Nevertheless, the **Musée de Pont-Aven** in the place de l'Hôtel de Ville (open Jul and Aug 10am–7pm daily; rest of year 10am–noon, 2–6pm) provides a glimpse into the landscape and traditions of Brittany, as well as a quick introduction to the works of the Pont-Aven school. You can see more of their works in the Musée des Beaux-Arts in Quimper *(see page 65)*. Art-lovers should buy a copy of the excellent book *Route des Peintres en Cornouaille*, which suggests itineraries for visiting the places that have inspired artists in this area.

From the Musée it's a short walk down to the tourist office where you should ask for their free guide to the forest walks and painting-spotting trails around Aven. Be sure to make the hour-long walk up through the Bois d'Amour to the exquisite **Trémalo chapel**, which still houses the gaunt yellow figure of Christ that featured in Gauguin's famous *Le Christe Jaune* of 1889.

Leave Pont-Aven by the D783, signposted to Quimperlé. At Riec-sur-Bélon turn right onto the D24 which weaves around the Bélon estuary, home of the famous Bélon oyster, to Clohars-Carnoët. Shortly after here turn right for Le Pouldu *plage* (D124).

Le Pouldu is where Gauguin and company moved to in the winter of 1889 and it has few of the tourist trappings that have overwhelmed Pont-Aven. Apart from its peaceful setting, the main reason for a visit here is to see the **Maison Marie Henry**, a diligent reconstruction of the inn where Gauguin, Sérusier, Bernard, Filiger and others stayed (rue des Grands-Sables, open Apr and May weekends 3–6pm; Jun and Sep

oose by Gauguin, Maison Marie Henry

Le Pouldu

Wed–Mon 3–7pm; Jul and Aug daily 10.30am–12.30pm and 3.15–7pm). Known as the 'Buvette de la Plage' its actual site was next door (now the Café de la Plage) but the museum maintains an authentic air: in the dining room, where the walls were playfully decorated by the artists, there are two original works – a wistful angel by Filiger and a white goose by Gauguin.

Leave Le Pouldu heading north for Quimperlé (D49), a delightful ride through the Forêt de Carnoët. At Quimperlé, cross the River Laïta and take the D22 to Plouay. Pass through Plouay, turning left as you leave the town onto the minor D178, signposted to Kernascléden, which runs along the edge of the Forêt de Pont-Calleck.

Brittany is a land that can seem tiresomely over-stocked with churches, but the one at **Kernascléden** is certainly worth seeing. A fine example of a small village cradling a large religious edifice at its centre, Kernascléden's church was built in 1453 by the Rohan family. Its grey-green granite, tamed by masons and adulterated by weather, may well be text-book Brittany but the slim tower, rose windows and stone-vaulted interior testify to the efforts of the builders to make this one something special.

Inside, apart from some striking paintings on the ceiling, to your right you'll find the scene painters' contribution: faded frescoes depicting the Dance of Death and a Hell where sinners are flayed, boiled and blinded as a preliminary to being chewed by grinning devils, mangled in barrels and skewered by trees.

Suitably cautioned, continue along the D782 to Guémené-sur-Scorff and turn left onto the D18

Hotel in Le Pouldu

to **Mur-de-Bretagne** via Cléguérec. Park in the place de l'Église, where there is a Pavillon du Tourisme. The *crêperie* **Les Blés d'Or** next door is a spotlessly clean restaurant popular with the locals, ideal for a light meal and a perusal of the day's *Ouest-France*.

You'll find Mur-de-Bretagne is an easy-going inland resort, perfect for walking and outdoor activities on and around the large Lac de Guerlédan *(see page 91)*.

Morbihan: Vannes to Paimpont

This itinerary takes you into the quiet forests and valleys of inland Brittany, travelling along back roads to medieval ruins and castles and to the ancient woods of Brocéliande, long known as a setting for Arthurian legends.

It begins in the lively city of **Vannes**, Brittany's medieval capital *(see page 71)*. Escaping it is not easy – look for signs to Ploërmel or Redon (not Josselin), for you need to get onto the N166 going east. About 10km (6 miles) from Vannes you turn left (N166) towards Elven. Shortly after this junction look for a turning left signposted 'Forteresse de Largoët', its entrance marked by two stone pillars. Better known as the **Tours d'Elven** (open Jun–Sep daily 10.30am–6.30pm; Mar–May and Oct weekends and hols 2–6.30pm),

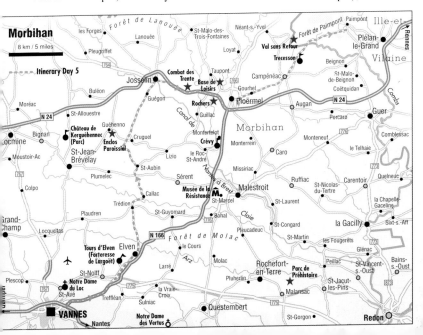

Tours d'Elven

this former castle is now an impressive ivy-clad ruin that can still evoke the thud of history. Drive on to its main entrance gate and park; from here it's a 25-minute walk through chestnut woods to the castle.

Begun in 1236 the castle was rebuilt in the 15th century by the Marshal de Rieux, one of Duke François II's officers. It was all but razed to the ground in 1488 by Charles VIII as punishment for François' part in an attempt to overthrow him. Today only two of an original eleven towers remain – a round tower, now partly restored, and the imposing six-storey keep. Rising spectacularly to 44m (144ft), the keep's lower walls are as thick as 9m (29ft) in places – looking up from the interior (beware dive-bombing pigeons) you can still see the huge fireplaces and stairways of this medieval skyscraper.

A genuine damsel-in-distress prison, the Tours d'Elven are said to have played host to a future English king, Henry VII, held captive here in 1474. They were also the setting of a popular 19th-century romantic novel by Octave Feuillet, *Roman d'un Jeune Homme Pauvre* (yes, the hero jumps from the tower to prove his love for the young girl imprisoned in the keep).

Return to the N166 and continue into the village of Elven, turning left on its outskirts (D1) for Trédion. This minor road takes you into the **Landes de Lanvaux**, once moorland but now a fertile and wooded upland with scattered settlements. In the 1790s the Chouans set up an independent kingdom here and in World War II it was a frequent place of refuge for the Resistance. Keep on the D1 until Trédion, then take the D133 to **Callac**, where you turn left to-

Josselin Castle

wards St Aubin. **Callac's church** has a calvary with particularly expressive faces; on the outskirts you will pass an elaborate grotto, a copy of the one at Lourdes. A little further on a small restaurant, the **Moulin de Callac**, provides the chance for a drink and a *crêpe* in the peace of the countryside.

Continue to St Aubin, past the church and on north towards Cruguel, turning left at an unsigned T-junction to join the D126 to **Josselin**. Piled up on the banks of the River Oust, this medieval town has long been overwhelmed by the mighty bulk of Josselin castle. As you draw near you'll see its steep walls greeting you with solid defiance – don't be daunted, for as you cross the bridge and climb up into the town you'll find it's just a façade – only three towers of its original nine survive today, the rest pulled down by Cardinal Richelieu in 1629 .

Try to park at the top of the town near the basilica Notre Dame du Roncier (but not on a Saturday, which is market day). From here it's a short walk to the town's attractive half-timbered hub, the place Notre Dame. For a light lunch try the **Bar-Crêperie du Centre** in the square; for something more substantial consider the **Hôtel de France**, also on the square, or the **Auberge de Clisson** (just up from the basilica).

To visit the **castle** cut through the slim rue du Château to its main entrance in place de la Congrégation, next to the Tourist

Josselin castle's impressive façade

Office. All visits are guided with some English commentary provided (open July to August 10am–6pm; June and September 2–6pm; April to May and October Wed, Sun and hols 2–6pm). The **exterior façade** is its most impressive feature – a tableau of ornamented granite that frequently incorporates the letter A, a tribute to the much-loved Duchess Anne. The interior, much of it restored in the 19th century, is a pompous amalgam of the portraits, mottoes and logos of the Rohan family, the castle's owners since 1407, who are still in residence.

Visitors may well prefer the nearby **Musée de Poupées**, a doll museum housed in the castle's former stables (opening hours as above), which displays some 600 dolls, as well as numerous toys used to amuse the children of the Rohan family, from the ancient days of miniature silver tea-sets to the plastic *croissants* and TGV trains of today.

Spare some time for the **basilica** too, its exterior spiked with lewd, jutting gargoyles. Founded in the 11th century, it is dedicated to Our Lady of the Bramble Bush who is said to have been discovered under such a bush in the 9th century. On the opposite side of her white stone altar lies the beatific tomb of Oliver and Marguerite de Clisson – one-time owner and rebuilder of Josselin castle, he rose to become Constable of France in 1380; his brutality during the Hundred Years War earned him the title 'Butcher of the English'. The worshippers beneath the tomb were beheaded during the French Revolution.

From Josselin the itinerary continues east but lovers of art

Tomb of Oliver and Marguerite de Clisson

and the countryside may prefer to sneak off to the excellent modern sculpture park at **Kerguéhennec**. Set in the grounds of an elegant 18th-century château, it lies 16km (10 miles) southwest of Josselin (take the N24 to St Allouestre then go south on the D11). The sculpture park offers visitors an aesthetic treasure-hunt through avenues of trees dotted with works by sculptors from all over Europe, as well as a changing programme of contemporary exhibitions and concerts (open daily 10am–6pm; Jun–Sep till 7pm, closed Mon).

To resume the itinerary leave Josselin on the D129/N24 to Ploërmel. About 4km (2½ miles) out of town the road bisects around 'La Pyramide', a monument to commemorate the site of the **Combat des Trente** of 1351. The 'Battle of the Thirty' tried to settle a long-running feud between French and English factions garrisoned in the castles of Josselin and Ploërmel during the War of the Breton Succession. Each side sent 30 knights to contest their cause in what was billed as a tournament (it was officially a time of truce) but which became a famous day of chivalry and carnage recorded in Froissart's *Chronicles*. It ended with eight dead and many wounded – the Bretons were declared the victors but the war rumbled on for another thirteen years.

Combat des Trente monument

Continue on the N24, by-passing Ploërmel (follow the signs to Rennes), till you reach Campénéac on the D134. Turn left here onto the D312 for **Paimpont**, a slate-and-granite market town that is the natural centre for exploring the Forêt de Paimpont *(see page 92)*. If you plan to stay here the **Relais de Brocéliande** (tel: 02 99 07 84 94) is warm and friendly and has an enjoyable restaurant.

Kerguéhennec sculpture park

PICK & MIX

1. St Malo

St Malo is one of the most appealing of the Channel ports. Head for its granite-walled heart, known as the cité intra-muros. The city gets its name from Maclou, a Welsh monk who arrived here in the 6th century to spread Christianity. For centuries it was a fortified island, linked to the mainland by a causeway, from where the Malouins ruled the Rance and the high seas beyond.

In 1534 Jacques Cartier, born in nearby Rothéneuf, discovered the St Lawrence River, and it was from here that settlers sailed in 1698

View from St Malo's ramparts

to colonise the Iles Malouines, better known as Las Malvinas or The Falklands. In the 17th and 18th-centuries St Malo's corsairs regularly plundered the English, Dutch and Spanish fleets, their piracy proving so profitable that its shipowners could afford to build solid country mansions, known as *malouinières,* in the neighbouring town of St Servan *(see page 47).*

St Malo was severely bombed by the Allies in 1944 and what you see today is an impressive reconstruction of the old city, built mainly in 18th-century style. Restoration of the **Cathédrale St-Vincent** was not finally completed until 1972. However, some streets between the cathedral and the castle did survive; rue du Pélicot still has its original wooden façades. Park outside the city walls, either alongside the Port de Plaisance or in the Esplanade St Vincent where the Tourist Office (tel: 02 99 56 64 48) is located. The best way to see St Malo is to take a leisurely 2-km (1½-mile) walk around its ramparts: they appear stern and fore-

boding at first but as the tide retreats you'll discover golden beaches nestling at their feet. You get up to the **ramparts** by some steps in the Porte St Vincent, to your left as you enter, but before you ascend them wander a short way up **rue Garangeau** (straight ahead from place Chateaubriand) and buy a cake or some chocolate to keep you going.

Make the walk clockwise, first passing by the pleasure boats in the **Bassin Vauban** and over the **Grande Porte**. Turn the corner at the **Bastion St Louis** where there is a statue of the gallant corsair René Duguay-Trouin (1673–1736). Down on the roundabout another of St Malo's famous sons is honoured: Mahé de la Bourdonnais (1699–1753), who took a leading role in the colonisation of Mauritius. As you near the next bastion, **St Philippe**, the views extend across the mouth of the Rance to Dinard. Here the long Môle des Noires stretches seawards and the power of the waves becomes more apparent: the tidal range around St Malo can be well over 10m (33ft).

The walk turns again to skirt the large **Bastion de la Hollande**: between here and the Tour Bidouane are some of the city's oldest ramparts dating from the Middle Ages, with Plage de Bon Secours below. As you continue round you will see the island of **Grand Bé**, which can be reached on foot at low tide. The writer François-

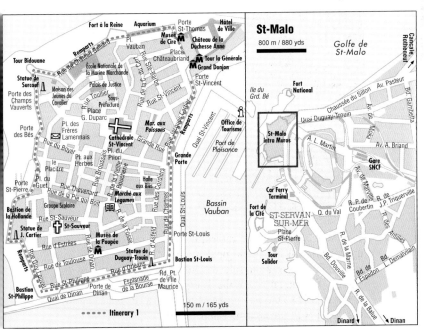

René de Chateaubriand

René de Chateaubriand (1768–1848), one of Brittany's best-known authors, is buried there. He was born in St Malo and his bizarre childhood at the family château in Combourg *(see page 105)* is chronicled in his *Mémoires d'Outre-Tombe*.

Next to the **Tour Bidouane** there is a small garden with a frantic statue of the corsair Robert Surcouf (1773–1827). Nearby is the Maison du Québec, a cultural centre fostering the age-old links between St Malo and Quebec in Canada. Turning the corner, the views are now east to Paramé and out to the Fort National, built in 1689 by Vauban and again only accessible at low tide.

The next bastion, **Fort à la Reine**, leads you back towards the Porte St Vincent and the steps down to place Châteaubriand. To your left you will see the towers and turrets of St Malo's **Castle**. It houses the city's **Musée d'Histoire de la Ville at du Pays Malouin**. The museum is most interesting for the insight it offers into the maritime adventures of local heroes like Cartier, Surcouf and Duguay-Trouin (open daily Apr–Sep 10am–noon and 2–6pm; low season closed Mon).

St Malo's Castle

Within the *cité* itself you'll find a cosy, cobbled network of narrow streets lined with expensive shops and more reasonably priced restaurants. If you are on your way home, St Malo is a perfect port of call for some last-minute shopping. Here you can pick up all those Breton artefacts you meant to buy but never did: for *faïence* try **Morly**, No. 6 rue Porcon de la Barbinais, and for folkloric souvenirs and *specialités régionales* visit the shops in rue Broussais. **Le Comptoir**, 5 rue des Merciers (just off the place de la Poissonnerie), has a useful range of mustards, pâtés, and liqueurs.

Eating out in St Malo is a far from arduous task. Rue Jacques Cartier offers visitors a good choice of pleasant pavement restaurants and in the side streets off it you'll find plenty of *crêperies*.

If you find life *intra-muros* getting a bit claustrophobic take yourself off to the quieter **St Servan**, just to the south, which has a good beach and the solid **Tour Solidor**, home to an unusual museum to the sailors of the Cape Horn (Apr to Oct 10am–noon and 2–6pm, low season closed Mon). Some of the exhibits here, such as the decorated rolling-pins given by mariners to loved ones, bear witty ditties that may explain why St Malo's explorers and privateers really put to sea:

"From rocks and sands and barren lands
  Kind fortune keep me free,
  And from great guns and women's tongues
  Good Lord deliver me."

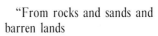

St Malo

Robert Surcouf

The Corsairs of St Malo

In the 17th-century St Malo was the largest port in France, a proud and impregnable island fortress whose privateers were the scourge of the oceans. Born of the long-running feuds between France and Britain, St Malo's corsairs were sponsored by the city's traders and *armateurs* (shipowners) and sanctioned by the state. They carried letters from the Crown, which licensed their activities in return for a share of the spoils; for this reason the people of St Malo have always preferred the term 'privateer' to 'pirate'.

Training for the priesthood appears to have been a good way to start a career in corsairing, followed by an early escape to sea. Two of St Malo's most famous maritime heroes followed this course, becoming captains of their vessels by the time they were 20. René Duguay-Trouin, born in 1673, was the tearaway son of a rich shipowner who set the piratical pace by capturing or sinking 85 English ships before he was 30. An aristocratic bandit who became chronically melancholic when on land, he was held captive in Plymouth for a year but escaped by boat. In 1711 he took Rio de Janeiro from the Portuguese and the following year quit the seas at the age of 36. This did not prevent him becoming a Lieutenant General in the French Navy, and he died in 1736 garlanded with honours.

Robert Surcouf, born a century later in 1773, graduated from slave-trading to piracy with an early coup, the seizure of the 150-strong HMS *Triton* with a force of only 18 men. His ships hounded the vessels of the East India Company in the Indian Ocean. The crowning exploit of his notorious career occurred in the Bay of Bengal in 1800 when he captured the 26-cannon HMS *Kent* in a famous David and Goliath naval engagement. He too retired at the age of 36. In due course he became a Baron of the French Empire and died in 1827, having become the richest shipowner in France.

2. Cancale

If you like oysters Cancale is the place to eat them. About 18km (11 miles) east of St Malo, this modest port has completely abandoned itself to the cultivation and enjoyment of these sensuous bivalves. Be sure to get there soon after noon to ensure a good choice of restaurants.

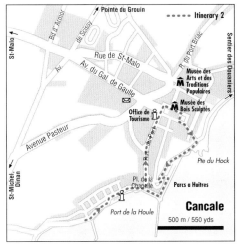

Leave St Malo heading east on the coastal road (D201) passing through the suburbs of Paramé to Rothéneuf. For an unusual diversion (20mins) look for a turning left as you pass through the centre of Rothéneuf signposted to **'Les Rochers Sculptés'**. This will take you down to a point in the cliffs where the rocks have been carved into a granite wonderland of faces, figures and creatures by a local priest, Abbé Fouré. He began work in 1870 and laboured for 25 years to produce some 300 carvings recounting the history and characters of the Rothéneuf family. Not all of the carvings have survived the ravages of time and tide, but if you spend a while there reading the rocks you'll find you're being watched by a lot more stony people than initial appearances suggest.

Les Rochers Sculptés

Granite face, Les Rochers Sculptés

The D201 continues out to the **Pointe du Grouin**, a breezy headland where the sea is often a truly emerald colour. From here there are fine views across the Baie du Mont St Michel to Normandy, the horizon pierced by its famous abbey. Nearby is the Ile des Landes, a bird sanctuary (guided walks Jul–Aug Tues–Sun, tel: 02 99 30 64 64 for details).

From Pointe du Grouin it's a short ride down into **Cancale** – turn left into the town centre and park by the church. From here you can walk downhill (rue du Port), passing the Tourist Office (tel: 02 99 89 63 72) to your right, to the port. Here fish restaurants stretch the length of the quayside with gaggles of lip-licking promenaders inspecting the menus outside.

If you plan to eat oysters and other seafood there's not much between them all, though some are considerably cheaper than others. **Le Narval** (20 Quai Gambetta, tel: 02 99 89 63 12) is a safe bet with *menus fixes* from around €17, which includes a choice of 10 *huîtres* (oysters). Cancale is also a good place to try a *plateau de fruits de mer* or local fish such as skate *(raie),* turbot or monkfish *(lotte)* – see 'Regional Specialities' in *Eating Out, page 94.*

The restaurants here also cater for gourmet tastes with five-course menus from €22 upwards and some gargantuan *menu gastronomiques* at around €33. Away from the hoi-polloi **Restaurant de Bricourt** (1 rue du Guesclin, tel: 02 99 89 64 76 – at the top of the town) occupies an early 19th-century house with a garden and Michelin-starred cuisine. If you like performance cookery take lots of money and book well ahead. At the other end of the scale you can have an equally regal meal at one of the open-air oyster bars along the port – here a few euros will set you up with a plate of oysters and a *demi-bouteille* of chilled Muscadet, a wine consumed in Cancale in vast quantities.

Cancale's oysters were famous even in Roman times and up until the 1850s they were simply collected wild from the Baie du Mont St Michel. Their strong flavour is said to derive from

Pointe du Grouin

Cancale oysters

the strong tides that wash over them daily. Today they are farmed commercially and if you walk out to the jetty at the eastern end of the port you can see the *parcs* where they are cultivated. Oysters spend four or five years in the water before they arrive on our tables: until the 1960s only flat oysters (*plates*, also known as Bélons) were cultivated here. Then a combination of severe winters and mysterious diseases decimated the population and now hollow oysters *(creuses)*, imported originally from Portugal (known as *portugaises*) but now from Japan (known as *gigas* but still also called *portugaises*) are farmed too.

The beds you can see (or half-see if the tide is in) represent only part of the cultivated area. Cancale oysters actually originate in the Gulf of Morbihan and neighbouring rivers, the year-old spat (embryo) being brought here to mature in deep-water beds. Later they are moved to shallower waters to be cleansed of mud and impurities – the basins you can see. It's worth walking down to the *parcs* to see the oyster-farmers at work; they are a hardy bunch whose lives are ruled by the tide, their cheery faces whipped ruddy by

Oyster culture in Cancale

mud, salt and wind. There are plenty of stalls selling this delicacy.

From here you can walk up onto the cliffs above and join the *Sentier des Douaniers* (Customs Officers' Path) that weaves around the coast back to the Pointe du Grouin. A short way along you will come to a small turning to your left (follow the signs to L'Église) which takes you back to the church and car park.

If you want to know more about the world of the oyster, Cancale has a small **museum** devoted to local arts and traditions housed in the former church of St Méen (open Jul and Aug daily except Mon morning 10am–noon and 2.30–6.30pm; Jun and Sep Thur–Sun 2.30–6.30pm). There is also **La Ferme Marine de Cancale**, on the Route de la Corniche as you head out from the port towards Les Portes Rouges, which is open for guided visits in English (daily at 2pm Jun–Sep; tel: 02 99 89 69 99). A little further round the Baie du Mont St Michel at **Le Vivier-sur-Mer** is France's principal centre for mussel-farming *(see page 84)*.

Plateau de fruits de mer

3. Dinan

Set high on a hill overlooking the Rance valley, Dinan obligingly fulfils the dream of what a French town should be like. The outskirts may be modern and chaotic but at its heart you'll find a delightful medieval shopping centre lined with half-timbered houses.

Dinan has all the well-heeled bustle of a market-town, which thankfully saves it from becoming too picturesque. Park, if you can, in the large **place du Guesclin** (but not on a Thursday which is market day). Just south of the square, on rue du Château, is the Tourist Office (tel: 02 96 87 69 76). A statue of Dinan's favourite son, Bertrand du Guesclin, disdainfully surveys the parked cars that now assemble on what was, in his day, a medieval fairground. Ugly and uncouth, Du Guesclin (1314–80) rose to become Constable of France and one of its greatest warriors: his methods were unchivalrous, mercenary and extremely successful – it was he who was responsible for expelling the English from France during the Hundred Years War. In 1359 in the adjacent place du Champ he fought and won a duel against the English knight, Thomas of Canterbury.

From the place du Guesclin walk through the rue Ste Claire, turning left into the rue de l'Horloge. You are now back in the Middle Ages, all credit cards accepted. Look out for the **Maison du Gisant**,

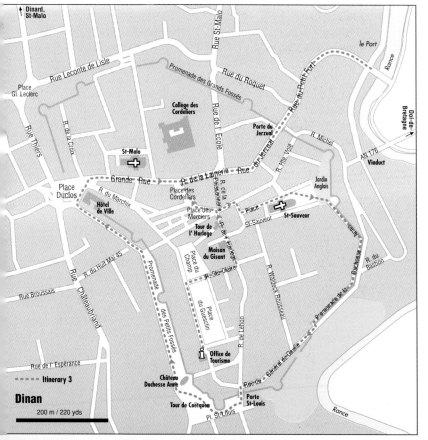

Dinan
200 m / 220 yds

Basilica St Sauveur

which has an arcaded porch beneath which lies a headless tombstone discovered during restoration. Further on you reach the 15th-century **Tour de l'Horloge** (clock tower), once the town hall. From the top are good views over Dinan's steep-roofed houses to the surrounding countryside (tower open Apr and May 2–6pm; Jun–Sep 10am–7pm, but avoid going on the hour unless you want to be deafened by the bells).

You'll find Dinan's street-names provide a good indication of how the town once earned its living. The rue de l'Horloge (Clock Street) veers left to become the place des Merciers (Haberdashers) and then the place des Cordeliers (Franciscan monks). Turn onto rue de la Lainerie (Woolshops), then right again along the rue de la Poissonnerie (Fishmongers), from where you can walk via the rue de la Larderie (Baconsellers) to the **Basilica St Sauveur**.

Begun in the 12th century, the basilica is refreshingly asymmetrical and undoubtedly one of Brittany's finest Romanesque churches. In the centre of the church you'll find a tombstone containing the heart of du Guesclin. That is all you will find too, for the rest of Dinan's hero is scattered between here and the Languedoc. After his death in 1380 at Châteauneuf-de-Randon his corpse underwent a macabre return journey. After being embalmed the entrails were buried at Le Puy (near Lyon), but this was so poorly done the flesh had to be removed and buried at Montferrand (in the

Dinan's rooftops from the clock tower

Dordogne), at which point the king intervened and ordered the skeleton be taken to the Basilica St Denis in Paris.

St Sauveur is set in a pleasant square where two pavement cafés, **L'Absinthe** and the **Hostel du St Sauveur** offer a chance for a drink and a light *plat du jour*. Alternatively you may prefer to give in to one of Dinan's irresistible *charcuteries* and take a *tarte à l'oignon* or some *bouchées fruits de mer* (seafood vol-au-vents) to the **Jardin Anglais** behind the basilica. From these gardens, which are adjacent to a 17th-century convent (now a retirement home), you can look out over the wooded banks of the Rance valley and down to Dinan's old port.

From here the itinerary takes you on an easy walk along and beside Dinan's ramparts (45mins) – if you prefer to omit this you can cut back through to the rue du Jerzual and walk down to the port *(see below)*. To start the walk turn right at the bottom of the Jardin Anglais into the **Promenade de la Duchesse Anne**, shaded with beech trees. This traces the route of the town's old ramparts, which peter out unhelpfully when you reach the busy rue du Général de Gaulle. Continue up the hill till you reach the Porte St Louis; just past it is the 15th-century **Tour de Coëtquen**. This is part of

the Château Duchesse Anne, which houses a **museum** of local history (open Jun–mid-Oct 10am–6.30pm daily; mid-Mar–May and mid-Oct–mid-Nov Wed–Sun 10am–12pm and 2–6pm; winter 1.30–5.30pm, closed Tues and Jan; entrance on rue du Château next to the tourist office).

From here you can go through the Porte St Louis and walk down the Promenade des Petits Fossés with Dinan's massive ramparts for company. Continue past a children's playground and mini-golf (Jardin du Val Cocherel) to the

Rue de Jerzual

place Duclos, where you can re-enter the old town via the Grande Rue. This leads you past St Malo's **church**, started in the late 15th-century but only completed in 1865 after being desecrated during the French Revolution. A harmonious mix of modern and 15th-century stained-glass windows creates a calm, sun-dappled ambience.

Grande Rue leads into the rue de la Lainerie then into Dinan's most photogenic street, **rue du Jerzual**. Steep and winding with timbered houses all askew and heavy with geraniums and sagging wooden balconies, this was once the main route into Dinan from the port. Your descent passes through the 14th-century **Porte du Jerzual** into the rue du Petit Fort, from where huge loads of cloth made by local weavers were once shipped.

Today the **port** is a quiet backwater mainly used by pleasure craft. If you fancy a quiet jaunt upriver, boats can be hired for the day from the port, tel: 06 07 45 89 97. To get back to the town you can either walk back up rue du Jerzual or hitch a ride on the *petit train* that passes by in summer time. For a longer walk back along the river (1hr 30mins) cross the bridge and turn right onto a towpath that follows the river round to Léhon, where you'll find the ruins of a 17th-century abbey, St Magloire. From here you can climb back up rue Beaumanoir to the Porte St Louis.

For shopping in Dinan try the **Cave des Jacobins** (3 rue Ste Claire) which sells Rance valley cider and Breton liqueurs. There are also several shops near here selling *faïence* and antiques, while **Au Rouet** in the rue de l'Horloge sells *broderie bretonne* and locally made table-linen and lace. On this street you'll also find plenty of tempting *crêperies*. Dinan's weaving and craft traditions are continued today in crafts shops along rue du Jerzual, which sell modern and traditional works in glass, wood, leather and ceramics.

4. Parish Closes

'Les enclos paroissiaux' are an eloquent expression of Breton Catholicism. Most of them are in northern Finistère with a concentration around the Elorn valley. This itinerary takes you to three of the best: it begins at St Thégonnec, 12km (7½ miles) southwest of Morlaix, which can be reached quickly via the N12 or in a more leisurely way by the D712.

Parish closes (walled-in or enclosed areas of hallowed ground) share common characteristics that each village has interpreted in its own way. All are absurdly large for the small rural settlements that surround them, for they were built at a time when Brittany had few urban centres but a considerable disposable wealth derived from maritime trade, flax production and the weaving of cloth. Most were commenced in the mid-16th century and completed in stages over the following two hundred years, elaborate works of devotion born of an intense religious faith and a keen inter-village rivalry.

There are three essential features: a triumphal arch or gateway marking your entry into the sacred ground surrounding the church; a calvary representing scenes from the Passion and Crucifixion, and an ossuary beside the church entrance housing bones exhumed from the adjacent cemetery when space was needed. These structures are vitalised and

St Thégonnec's calvary

embellished with coarse stone carvings, stern and unyielding granite being the only raw material available for this monumental poetry, now so often movingly reworked by weather. Each ensemble thus achieves several purposes: it serves as a didactic Bible writ large in cartoons of stone, it acts as a tangible bridge between the living and the dead, and it represents a communal act of homage that supercedes the passing of generations.

St Thégonnec

This is the most famous of the parish enclosures, built over many years as parish funds permitted. Enter through the **triumphal arch** (1587); to your left is the **ossuary** (1676–82). In the **crypt** below is a sepulchral scene depicting Mary Magdalen's sorrow (1702). Ahead of you rises the **calvary** (1610). Here the craftsmen's work,

St Thégonnec's triumphal arch

raised to a humbling but accessible height and silhouetted against the heavens, sings of the fervent desire of a Breton village to honour the tragedy and serenity of Christ's humiliation. First you see Christ blindfolded and tormented, then (walking in an anti-clockwise direction) the flagellation, the carrying of the Cross, and finally the Crucifixion. In a niche below this there is a statue of St Thégonnec with a cart pulled by wolves – harnessed up after they ate his donkey.

The church has a Renaissance **tower** modelled on that at Pleyben with another image of St Thégonnec above the porch. Statues of the Apostles oversee your entry into the nave where the principal attraction is a carved **pulpit** (1683) depicting the Cardinal Virtues. Brightly painted and lined with busy 18th-century woodcarvings, the interior is in stark contrast with the simple, animated scenes outside.

Back in lay territory you will find a couple of *boulangeries* that can administer to your bodily needs, while the **Auberge St Thégonnec** (tel: 02 98 79 61 18), also a hotel, has an excellent restaurant serving local dishes.

When you leave, take the D712 towards Kermat, where you turn left for Guimiliau.

Guimiliau

Here the architecture is on a smaller but even more remarkable and endearing scale. Once more there is a triumphal arch, with a calvary to the right of the church and beyond it a funereal chapel. The **calvary** (1581–8) is the most intense in Brittany, and described with typical Breton severity in the church's companion notes as 'granite with secular lichen'. There are nearly 200 figures adorning it, a lively crowd with billowing moustaches and histrionic grimaces, many of them wearing 16th-century dress.

The statues are on two levels, the lower section somewhat sober and rigid, the top vigorous and dynamic. Amongst the customary scenes from the Passion (in no chronological order) is a cautionary illustration of a local Breton legend, the torment of Katell Gollet (Catherine the Damned). Katell's crime was to steal a consecrated wafer in order to please her lover (the Devil in disguise), for which she was despatched to Hell to be tortured by demons. Her demise is graphically depicted above the Last Supper, a warning to all flirtatious women.

The **funereal chapel** (1648) has an exterior pulpit originally used for open-air sermons on All Souls' Day, an occasion that must have made an extraordinary medieval scene. To the left of the church entrance is the ossuary. The church itself, with its leaning tower, looks somewhat unstable – above the porch is a statue of St Miliau, a King of Cornouaille who was beheaded by his evil brother. The **porch** (1606–17), the traditional place of assembly for the parish council, is a masterpiece, with its orbiting angels and parade of faded wooden

The Auberge St Thégonnec

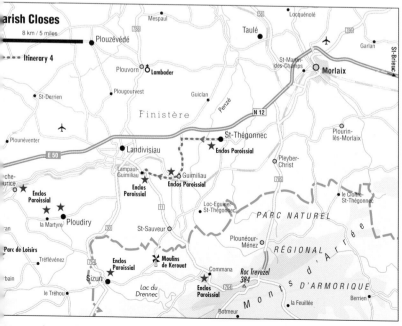

Guimiliau's calvary

and stone Apostles. The interior is also rewarding, with a 17th-century organ unsteadily supported by slender wooden columns and an octagonal carved oak baptistry (1675).

Beyond the church walls the *crêperie* **Ar Chupen** reminds us of more mundane pleasures. Just opposite, in the simple bar-cum-shop Le Relais du Calvaire, you can have a drink and a snack and play a game of pool.

When you leave Guimiliau, take the D111, heading down the hill to Lampaul-Guimiliau.

Lampaul-Guimiliau

As you near this parish close you'll notice the church has a wounded demeanour, the result of a lightning strike which demolished part of its spire in 1809, reducing its height by 18m (60 ft). Enter the close through its monumental gate (1669) – to the left is the chapel and ossuary (1667), to the right a simple calvary.

This time it is the **church**, commenced in 1609, that steals the show. Above the entrance is a statue of St Pol with St Michael below; the **porch** (1533) is guarded by the traditional Twelve Apostles. The church interior is richly decorated with brightly coloured paintings and elaborate wood carvings. Scenes from the Passion are portrayed along the rood-beam separating the nave from the choir, while on the 17th-century Altarpiece of the Passion the birth of the Virgin Mary and the martyrdom of the headless St Miliau are depicted in painted wood panels. Look out also for the faded gilt banners of St Pol (1634) and the Virgin (1667), now displayed in cases but which are still paraded annually when Lampaul-Guimiliau holds its *pardon*.

More Parish Closes

If you're keen to see more, there are plenty more *enclos paroissiaux* in the surrounding area. Travelling anti-clockwise from Lampaul-Guimiliau you'll find them at La Roche-Maurice

Church in Lampaul-Guimiliau

(where there is a threatening depiction of Ankou, the Breton embodiment of Death), La Martyre (the oldest of them all), Ploudiry, Sizun (which has a magnificent triumphal arch) and Commana. You can also pick up a leaflet from Tourist Offices outlining a *circuit des enclos paroissiaux*. Further afield there are outstanding parish closes at Pleyben (near Châteaulin, one of the largest in Brittany), Plougastel-Doulas and, surprisingly adrift from all these, a calvary at Guéhenno (near Josselin).

5. Roscoff

Few holiday-makers visited Roscoff before it became a Channel port and there's no need to make a special trip to see it. However if you're one of the 530,000 visitors who catch a ferry here each year you'll find it's a pleasant place to while away some time.

The old port of Roscoff lies to the west of the modern deep-water harbour and ferry terminal. A long seafront curves round the bay with the Tourist Office (tel: 02 98 61 12 13) housed in a former chapel, bang in the middle. Leading north from here a back street, the rue Gambetta, provides a popular opportunity for some last-minute shopping before heading for home. For local specialities try the *poissonnerie* **Maron** (No. 28), which sells jars of its home-made *soupe de poissons,* while a little further on in rue Amiral Réveillère the *pâtisserie* **Alain Guyader** sells Breton liqueurs, cakes and chocolates. In the same street (No. 1) **Rosko Goz** stocks stripey

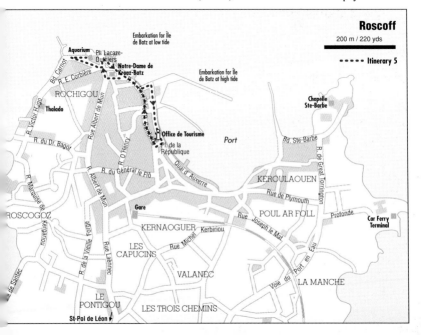

Roscoff old port

Breton T-shirts, fishermens' sweaters, dufflecoats and sailing gear. Roscoff's back streets also reveal its history. Rue Amiral Réveillère runs into the triangular place Lacaze Duthiers where a few granite façades remain from the 16th- and 17th-century shipowners' mansions that were once a grand feature of the port. Like St Malo, Roscoff has a piratical past and the coast west of here was once notorious for the cliff-top bonfires lit by the locals as false beacons intended to lure foreign ships onto the rocks.

If you look at the thick granite walls of the church **Notre Dame de Kroaz Batz** opposite, you'll see cannons decorating the tower and a weather-beaten sailing ship cruising over the porch. The church was begun in 1515 but is still in a Gothic style – architectural fashions, like everything else, took a long time to reach Finistère. However, the lantern belltower (1550–76) has a Renaissance grace.

As you enter the church look to your right where there is a Gallo-Roman **font** used for total-immersion baptisms. The unembellished interior still has a feeling of 16th-century austerity – its most notable feature is a series of 15th-century alabaster panels depicting the Passion – there were seven but three were stolen in 1981.

In the far corner of the place Lacaze Duthiers a narrow street takes you to the fortress-like **Charles Pérez Aquarium** (open Apr–Oct daily 2–6pm; Jun–Aug daily 10am–noon and 2–6pm) which has a collection of over 300 aquatic specimens from the Channel. Other diversions can be found back by the port's main jetty: a *petit train* offers a tour of the town; there are also frequent trips to the **Ile de Batz** *(see page 78)*. The Chapelle Ste-Barbe provides good views of the town and port, while on the other side of the ferry terminal the **Tropical Gardens** (open Jun–Sep 10am–7pm; reduced hours rest of year; tel: 02 98 61 29 19) offer colourful and exotic floral evidence of Roscoff's mild climate. To the west of the old port, on rue Victor Hugo,

General view of Roscoff

the 'Thalado' discovery centre gives a free introduction to the astonishing world of seaweed. Roscoff claims to be the birthplace of thalassotherapy (therapy using marine products) and has two centres *(see page 107)*.

The best sandy beach near to Roscoff is to the west of the old port at **Laber** and there are even better ones beyond Plouescat. Roscoff is not a place to splash out on an expensive meal, but there are many welcoming cafés and *crêperies* around the old port. If you like big old seaside hotels try the cavernous seaview restaurant in the **Hôtel des Arcades** (15 rue Amiral Réveillère).

6. Quimper

A leisurely walk around the old market town of Quimper.

'A charming little place' Flaubert called Quimper, and it's hard to disagree. Founded by St Corentin some time between the 4th and 7th centuries, the city developed around the confluence (*kemper* in Breton) of the Steir and Odet rivers to become the ancient capital of Cornouaille. Today it's Brittany's most Celtic city where specialist

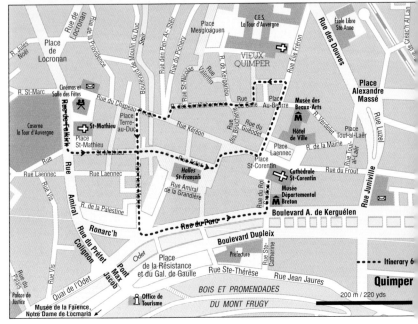

shops sell traditional costumes, keltia musique and Breton-language books. Quimper's citizens celebrate their Welsh and Cornish ancesty proudly every July with a great Celtic shindig, the Fêtes du Cornouaille *(see page 114)*.

Quimper sprawls – an endearing feature that contributes to its relaxed and unpretentious atmosphere. If you're coming from the north try to park near the church of St Mathieu in the rue de Falkirk. There's also a large car park near the River Odet close to the Tourist Office (tel: 02 98 53 04 05) on place de la Résistance. From either spot it's a short walk to the pedestrianised sanctuary of Vieux Quimper. If you arrive in the morning make straight for the **Halles St François** (straight ahead), a covered market open

Café sign: King Gradlon

Monday to Saturday. Quimper's old market burnt down in 1976 and its replacement is a bright, airy building with huge roof-beams like an inverted boat. Look out for stalls selling honey and *hydromel* (mead) from Quéménéven and be sure to visit a *boulangerie* here to buy a piece of *far breton* (custard flan with prunes) or a sticky *kouign amann*.

From the market you can turn left up rue St François into the main shopping street, rue Kéréon, then walk right towards Quimper's imposing cathedral, **St Corentin**. It dates from 1240 but has been ceaselessly altered ever since, the latest addition being the spires in 1856. One unusual feature is the way the choir is placed at an angle to the nave. The exterior craftily conceals this deviance but you will be able to spot a statue of King Gradlon on horseback set between the two spires of the west front.

King Gradlon is Quimper's mythical founder, once ruler of the coastal kingdom of Ys, which was protected by a dyke. The Devil, disguised as a handsome young man, tricked his wayward daughter into opening the keys to the city, thus flooding his kingdom. Gradlon escaped on horseback with his daughter clinging on, but the voice of God ordered him to jettison her, at which point the seas retreated. Gradlon moved inland and founded Quimper. His picture appears on the tourist board logo.

Around the cathedral and the place St Corentin there are often stalls selling lace and Breton souvenirs; in one corner of the square you'll find the **Café du Finistère**, a good meeting point where you can sit and watch the Quimperois go by. Nearby you'll see a statue of René-Théophile Laënnec (1781–1826), inventor of the stethoscope. It stands outside the excellent **Musée des Beaux-Arts**, which houses a collection of European paintings and drawings from the 16th century onwards (open Jul and Aug 10am–7pm, rest of year 10am–noon and 2–6pm; closed Tues and Sun am).

Apart from the outstanding quality of many of the works in the collection the most interesting aspect of the museum is the historical insight it offers into Breton life. Here you can still find that romantic, mystical Brittany of popular imagination which is probably half the reason so many people come to the region – a Bretagne of bustling markets and back-breaking toil in the fields, of lonely calvaries and solemn *pardons,* stormy seascapes and sacred woods. The collection is strongest in late 19th- and early 20th-century works (the Pont-Aven school, except Gauguin, is well represented) but it also introduces modern Quimper-born artists

Vieux Quimper

Hand-painted faïence

such as Max Jacobs and Pierre de Belay.

Quimper's other main attractions are shopping, café-hopping and *faïence*. For shopping, venture up the rue Élie Fréron into Vieux Quimper, a network of quiet streets with small designer boutiques and shops selling antiques and *brocante*. Look out for **No. 8** in this street where you can buy all the pans and utensils to start your own mini-*crêperie* when you get home. The proprietor will even give you some recipes to start you off and the shop also sells cider bowls and jugs. From here you can cut left through to the rue des Gentilshommes and back down to the river. For Breton music try **Keltia Musique** in the delightful place au Beurre.

The rue du Parc is where you'll find two of Quimper's more up-market riverside (and traffic-side) cafés, the **Café de l'Épée** and the **Grand Café de Bretagne**. The latter is also a *brasserie* where you can eat on a scale to suit your appetite. Quimper is not really a place for lavish dining but one for snacks and cheap meals – have an omelette here and a *plat du jour* there – you'll find more bars and restaurants if you wend your way towards the railway station or go across the river towards the allées de Locmaria. The **Crêperie au Vieux Quimper** (20 rue Verdelet, closed Tuesdays) is one of the most popular and there are more good *crêperies* in the place au Beurre and the surrounding streets. A little more expensive but still excellent value is **Le Jardin d'Eté**, 15 rue du Sallé, which serves delicious French food.

For *faïence*, the tin-glazed earthenware that is Quimper's distinctive speciality, two shops have good selections: **Art de Cornouaille** (12 place St Corentin) and **La Civette** (16 bis rue du Parc). It is not cheap but nearby factories sell seconds, and you can take a guided tour (30mins) around the workshops.

Faïence has been made in Quimper since 1690. The pottery was originally produced to meet local needs, for example as wedding presents and heirlooms, but now it is exported to collectors all over the world. Today, machinery is used to make the pottery but the designs are still hand-painted, the decoration being applied to the piece before the final firings. The nearest factory is **HB-Henriot**, past the tourist office, south of the river Odet on rue Haute (open all year Mon–Fri guided tours only 9.15am–5pm). **Musée de la Faïence**, at 14 rue J. B. Bousquet, traces the history of this craft (open 15 Apr–31 Oct Mon–Sat 10am–6pm).

HB-Henriot faïence factory sign

The mysterious stones at Carnac

7. Carnac

Carnac is one of the world's great prehistoric sites. There are exactly 2,792 menhirs (standing-stones) protruding from the heathland to the north of this seaside town.

Most of Carnac's standing-stones are in neat, parallel rows *(alignements)* that stretch for over 3.8km (2 miles), erected by a highly organised and industrious race any time between 5000 and 1800BC. Some will be fascinated by these perplexing megaliths; others will find them distinctly unimpressive. Many have been fenced off to prevent erosion and damage.

If you're approaching from the north try to arrive via minor roads, taking the D186 south (which you can join at Kergroix) till you reach the D196, where you turn right onto the Route de Kerlescan, which leads into the **'Route des Alignements'** and Carnac ville. This back route provides the most dramatic introduction to the megaliths – it may be crawling with traffic but the more slowly you drive the longer you will get to see them. You will pass three main groups – the Alignements de Kerlescan, the Alignements de Kermario (the largest and most impressive) and, after you've crossed the D119, the Alignements du Ménec.

Megaliths, Carnac

Looking at the menhirs of Carnac one soon appreciates the precision with which these immense stones have been placed. Whoever erected them had a clear purpose, a high degree of engineering skill and a huge workforce. Similar megalithic structures have been found elsewhere in Europe but never in such large numbers or in such a large-scale pattern as here.

History has not helped us in our puzzling. It is clear that once there were many more stones here, perhaps even twice as many. Erosion, earthquakes and man's pillaging have all disfigured the original design, with stones being destroyed by builders, removed by farmers and repositioned by well-intentioned but amateur archaeologists. Not that this has prevented hundreds of experts from finding pattern in their madness. Close surveying and statistical analysis has now made it clear that the *alignements* have a thoroughness of design not readily apparent to the eye of the casual visitor. The menhirs are not spaced equally, but grow closer together towards their outer rows. At the same time the rows converge fan-like as they move eastwards, and the size of the individual stones increases. Sometimes the rows take a bend northwards, sometimes they are not rows but parallel curves. All this could imply a central axis, and indeed one has been nominated, the Grand Menhir at Locmariaquer. Perhaps all the megaliths scattered around Morbihan were part of a large network designed, say, to plot the movements of the moon and stars.

Many people feel that the *alignements* do form part of some primitive calculator, perhaps for recording or deducing astronomical data, perhaps simply as a diary for the seasons to aid farmers. Others attribute a deeper religious significance: perhaps the stones are an act of worship, a message from the living to the dead, or a zodiac temple. Folklore offers other suggestions: the stones, phallic-shaped and erected at angles, were anointed with honey, wax and oil as part of fertility rituals in which infertile women would slide down them. Perhaps they were part of annual communal festivals, with a new stone erected each year to the light of nocturnal ritual fires and sacrificial ceremonies. This might explain why over the centuries many Christians have called for the destruction of the stones, and why elsewhere they have been capped with crosses.

Or maybe it doesn't. Perhaps Flaubert is right after all: 'Carnac' he declared, 'has had more rubbish written about it than it has standing stones.'

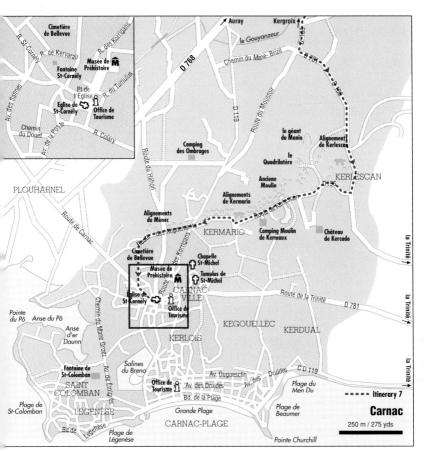

A good way to enjoy Carnac is by hiring a bicycle from shops like Lorcy, 6 rue de Courdiec (in Carnac-Ville) or Cyclo Tours, 89 avenue des Druides (in Carnac-Plage). You will need your passport or credit card as a deposit.

Don't bother going to Archéoscope, a pretentious audio-visual show about the megaliths by the Alignements du Ménec, but be sure to visit the **Musée de Préhistoire** in the place de la Chapelle in Carnac-Ville (open Jun–Sep Mon–Fri 10am–6.30pm, weekends and hols 10am–noon and 2–6.30pm; Oct May daily except Tues 10am–noon and 2–6.30pm). This is a far from dull affair which sets Carnac's megaliths into the context of prehistory in an accessible way. Many of the contents excavated from the tumuli and dolmens in the area are displayed here, including some hauntingly beautiful primitive stone carvings. Explanatory booklets in English can be borrowed and the collection extends right up to the colonisation of Brittany by the Romans and Celts.

If you get the megalith bug the museum also has a useful book-shop with guides to the other 3,000 menhirs, dolmens and tumuli dotted around Morbihan. **Locmariaquer** nearby is another principal site where you can inspect 'Le Grand Menhir', the world's largest standing stone (20.3m/64ft) which is now, alas, broken into four

Asterix, popular Celtic cartoon hero

pieces. Masochists may also care to take a short guided journey into the interior of the extensive **Tumulus de St Michel** to the east of Carnac (closed for renovation in 2002; contact the tourist office for new opening times). It was probably erected around 5–4000BC and like all graves is dark, smelly and rather claustrophobic inside.

Carnac itself is divided into two parts: Carnac-Ville and Carnac-Plage. The **beach** here is a good long stretch of pale sand, one of the best in the area and therefore well attended. On the hill above it Carnac-Ville radiates out from the church of **St Cornély**, which has an unusual baroque stone canopy above its north entrance. The church is dedicated to St Cornelius, patron saint of horned animals, and it is worth venturing inside to see the scenes from his life painted on the central wooden vaults of the ceiling in the 1730s by an artist from Pontivy.

In medieval times Carnac was the focus of an important week-long *pardon* when all the local cattle would be brought to the church to be blessed – on rue St Cornély you can still see an 18th-century fountain used for this purpose. St Cornély inveighed against the pagan practice of animal sacrifice and was martyred for his views by the Romans. Legend says that the legionnaries chased him and his two oxen all the way from Rome to Carnac. On reaching the sea he turned upon his pursuers and transformed them to stone; these petrified warriors have puzzled archaeologists ever since.

In Carnac-Ville the **Tourist Office** in the place de l'Église (open April to October and hols) has maps and leaflets detailing short walks in the vicinity of Carnac. The main office (tel: 02 97 52 13 52) is in Carnac-Plage (74 avenue des Druides) open all year. The **Hôtel Marine**, 4 place la Chapelle, Tel: 02 97 52 07 33 (closed Jan–Feb), in Carnac-Ville has a brasserie and a restaurant, with local seafood a principal feature of its menus. The modern bar is lively and popular with locals. **Le Râtelier** (4 chemin du Douët, tel: 97 52 05 04), also a hotel, has a quieter, country-house ambience with excellent food but slow service.

Church of St Cornély

8. Vannes

If you arrive here after touring round western Brittany, where life is perpetually sensible and conservative, then Vannes will come as a welcome surprise. Being that bit closer to the body of France the city has a lively Gallic energy in keeping with its status as a former capital of the region.

Today, Vannes is a busy agricultural centre with all the horrendous development on the city's outskirts that this implies, but at its centre you will find one of the most enjoyable old towns in Brittany.

Vannes

If you're driving into town from the north, try to park in the place de la République just off the rue Thiers. Today this long street, which runs north–south, marks the western edge of the old town, with the remnants of Vannes' medieval ramparts bordering the east.

As you drive down rue Thiers you won't be able to miss the **Hôtel de Ville**, built in the 1880s and defended by an equestrian statue of Arthur de Richemont, the Breton Duke who defeated the English at the end of the Hundred Years War.

Continuing on rue Thiers from place de la République it is a short walk south to the Tourist Office (tel: 02 97 47 24 34), operating from a 17th-century townhouse known as the **Hôtel de Limur**, and thence round to Vannes' picturesque Port de Plaisance. Here, the **Porte St Vincent** (1704) marks the traditional gateway into the medieval town from the port, once a bustling harbour but now a canalised *cul-de-sac* frequented by pleasure craft, flanked by three large car parks (one of them free).

The pavement cafés in the adjacent place Gambetta offer a comfortable vantage point for watching Vannes go by and are a good opportunity to enjoy a coffee before touring the town.

Leave the place Gambetta and continue walking east round the side of the city walls and along the rue Le Pontois. The road runs beside Vannes' impressive ramparts, now well restored and still containing segments of the city walls constructed by the Romans in the 4th century.

Left, Vannes ramparts.
Right, the medieval quarter.

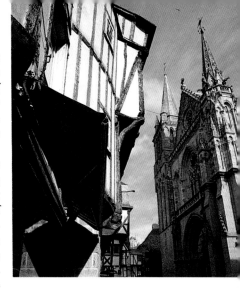

Vannes gets its name from the Veneti, the Celtic tribe whose sailing ships dominated the Gulf of Morbihan until a windless day in 56BC when a fleet of oar-propelled galleys commanded by Julius Caesar destroyed them.

It was from Vannes that the Romans built roads penetrating into all parts of Armorica. Later the city became the capital of the first Breton kingdom, proclaimed by Nominoë in the 9th century. There is a plaque here commemorating the final quashing of this idealistic dream: the Union of Brittany and France which the Duchess Anne signed here in 1532. Today Vannes' power has been usurped by Rennes and Nantes, climbing ivy scales its proud ramparts and floral gardens fill its broad moats.

For a far-reaching view of the ramparts and the medieval town beyond you can cross the road and climb up to the Promenade de la Garenne, which rejoins the rue Le Pontois a little further on. If you continue on the lower level you'll soon come to the **Porte Poterne**, where beneath the bridge there are some picturesque 17th-century washhouses *(anciens lavoirs)*. Further on you will pass the 15th-century Constable's Tower (Tour du Connétable) and then the 16th-century Powder Tower. The grand building on your right-hand side is the Préfecture, which was built in the 1880s.

Passing the Préfecture on your right, turn left into a narrow street that leads to Porte Prison and the old town. Climbing up the hill, veer to the right, around the back of the Cathédrale St

17th-century washhouses

Half-timbered houses in the medieval quarter

Pierre, along rue des Chanoines (canons) into the place Henri IV. Now you are in the centre of Vannes' *quartier médiéval,* a subtly restored confusion of cobbled streets and lop-sided half-timbered houses where for once the carefully inserted banks and designer shops do not deaden the authentic ring of history. As it happens, the most incongruous building here turns out to be the over-sized **Cathédrale St Pierre**, a veritable jigsaw of styles that architects have been fiddling with since the 13th century.

Inside the porch to the left you'll find a colour-coded plan revealing precisely what a jumble of ideas the place is. No doubt this makes it a godsend to lecturers in the history of ecclesiastical architecture but for the casual visitor only the Chapel of the Holy Sacrament (fourth *chapelle* on your left) is essential viewing. This contains the tomb of Vincent Ferrier, the Spanish saint to whom the cathedral is dedicated. Born in Valencia in 1350, St Vincent was a Dominican monk who spent a peripatetic life preaching all over Europe, arriving in Vannes only a year before his death in 1419. Such was St Vincent's popularity that the citizens refused both the Dominican and Spanish claims on his body, voting to restore their cathedral as a fitting home for his grave, which had since become a fount-head of miracles.

Opposite the entrance to the cathedral stands a former covered market and courthouse known as **La Cohue** (the throng or hub-bub). Many parts of the building date from the 13th century, which was also used as a theatre until 1940. Now it houses the **Musée des Beaux-Arts de Vannes**, an imaginatively displayed collection of art and artefacts relevant to the history of Vannes and past life in the Gulf of Morbihan (open mid-Jun–Sep daily 10am–6pm; rest of year 1.30–6pm).

Walk past La Cohue and into the rue des Halles, where you will find a useful delicatessen called **La Tapenade**. This stocks a good range of Breton specialities, including the local brew, *chouchen*. From here follow rue des Halles south into the place de Valencia where, from beneath the eaves of a 16th-century house jutt a merry couple carved in wood called, 'Vannes and his wife'.

Around the corner in the rue Noë is the **Musée d'Histoire et d'Archéologie** housed in the 15th-century Château Gaillard, once the seat of the Breton parliament. The museum contains finds from the megalithic sites in Morbihan including jewellery from Carnac and Locmariaquer (open daily Jun–Sep 10am–6pm).

From the place de Valencia take the narrow rue des Orfèvres (goldsmiths) back to the rue de la Monnaie. Walk down this into place des Lices, once a field where medieval tournaments and fairs were held. On Wednesday and Saturday mornings a market is held here and in the nearby place du Poids Public, with a separate fish market in place de la Poissonnerie. Further downhill rue St Vincent leads you back through the Porte St Vincent to place Gambetta.

For eating out, Vannes has plenty to offer its visitors, though within the old city walls prices can be on the steep side. **La Crêperie des Remparts**, 18 rue des Vierges, is an attractive option, with views of the ramparts from the terrace. Rue des Halles is lined with restaurants; **Arnaud Lorgéoux**, at No. 17, is worth considering for a mid-price meal, while for something upmarket venture up the rue de la Fontane (near the Église St Paterne) to **La Morgate**, which specialises in first-rate seafood.

For entertainment in Vannes, 1.6km (1 mile) south from the Port de Plaisance is the **Parc du Golfe**, a leisure complex that includes one of the largest bowling alleys in France. There is also a **Butterfly Conservatory** and an above-average **Aquarium**. Nearby at the Gare Maritime is the embarkation point for the boats that tour around the Gulf of Morbihan (*see page 85 for details*).

Place Valencia, 'Vannes and his wife'

EXCURSIONS...

9. Islands

A selection of spectacular islands that can be easily visited on a day trip from one of the coastal ports.

Brittany's jagged coast is dotted with islands. Most are small granite lumps inhabited by stubborn plants and visited only by seagulls, but there are a few spectacular exceptions. Some of these are only a stone's throw from the shore, like the island of Grand Bé off St Malo which at low tide can be reached by a short walk across the sands. Others are isolated rocks lost in the fogs and storms of the Atlantic, like the Ile d'Ouessant, France's most westerly point. Some are flat and austere but others have unspoilt wildlife, sandy beaches, hotels and an unexpectedly bucolic air. Fifteen are large enough to seduce a permanent population into living on them.

   In the summer months making the crossing to the islands can often mean turning up at a quay and boarding the next boat, though others will require prior reservation. If the weather's good, take a picnic so you can avoid the crowds and inflated prices.

   The **Ile de Bréhat** is one of the easiest islands to visit. It's also one of the most charming and could easily be incorporated into

Island ferry

your travels along the Côte de Granit Rose *(see page 25)*. It lies to the north of Paimpol and the embarkation point for the 15-minute crossing is the Pointe de l'Arcouest. The island, which is only 3.5km (2 miles) long, is really two islands, linked by a bridge known as the Pont ar Prad. The climate is surprisingly mild, allowing oleander, mimosa and a variety of fruit trees to flourish in the gardens and hedges that border its low, undulating fields.

Bréhat has a slightly comic air, like a rural Toytown, for cars are banned and the only ton-up vehicles permitted are baby tractors. Numerous small paths criss-cross the island allowing visitors to lose themselves with ease – be sure to climb up to the **Chapelle Saint-Michel** for a view of the whole island. You could easily spend a pleasant hour or an idle day on Bréhat (there are three hotels, often fully booked) but try to avoid going in the height of summer when it can get over-whelmed with tourists. If you push on to the north island things will be quieter. Bicycles can be hired from the main harbour, **Port Clos**, from where you can also take a one-hour boat tour round the island. Les Vedettes de Bréhat operate

Sea crossing

77

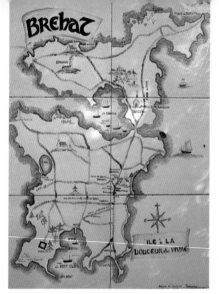

crossings to the island from Pointe de l'Arcouest all year (from 8.30am–8pm in July and August), tel: 02 96 55 79 50; www.vedettesdebrehat.com. Further information is available from the tourist office in Le Bourg, tel: 02 96 20 04 15.

Further west, to the north of Roscoff the **Ile de Batz** (Tourist Office, tel: 02 98 61 75 70) is a similar size to Bréhat but sparser, treeless and more windswept. A 15-minute crossing from the mainland, it is still warmed by the Gulf Stream and a mild climate allows the islanders to grow vegetables. Seaweed has long been harvested here – originally for fuel, now for fertiliser. There are two hotels, a campsite, sandy beaches and 14km (9 miles) of easy coastal walks. From Roscoff you can travel all year to Batz with Armein Excursions, tel: 02 98 61 77 75, and the Compagnie Finistérienne de Transport Maritime, tel: 02 98 61 78 87.

Getting to the **Ile d'Ouessant** (also known as Ushant), 30km (19 miles) west of the Brest peninsula, can be a rougher experience. Its hazardous waters are where the oil tanker Torrey Canyon went down in 1967, and the beam of its lighthouse at Créac'h, signalling the entrance to the English Channel, is one of the strongest in the world. There are crossings from Le Conquet (2¼ hours), Brest (1¼ hours) and, in summer, from Camaret (1 hour). You can also take the 15-minute flight on Finist'Air (tel: 02 98 84 64 87).

Ouessant is stormy and windswept in winter, besieged by migrating birds in spring and autumn, and pleasantly mild in summer. As part of the Parc Régional d'Armorique it is a birdwatcher's paradise and has two interesting sights: the **Eco-**

Rock pools, Ile de Bréhat

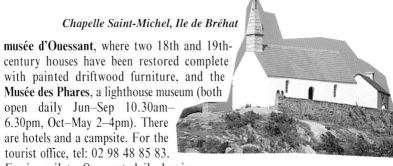

Chapelle Saint-Michel, Ile de Bréhat

musée d'Ouessant, where two 18th and 19th-century houses have been restored complete with painted driftwood furniture, and the **Musée des Phares**, a lighthouse museum (both open daily Jun–Sep 10.30am–6.30pm, Oct–May 2–4pm). There are hotels and a campsite. For the tourist office, tel: 02 98 48 85 83. Ferries sail to Ouessant daily leaving early in the morning; for times, contact the Compagnie Maritime Penn-ar-Bed (tel: 02 98 80 80 80; www.penn-ar-bed.fr) or Finist'Mer (tel: 02 98 89 16 61; www.finist-mer.fr). Some boats call in at the small but inhabited island of Molène.

The **Ile de Sein**, 5 miles (8km) west of the Pointe du Raz, is only just an island. Its bare, flat landscape rarely rises above 1.5m (5ft) and in the past it has almost been submerged. Today some 250 people struggle resolutely to live there, supporting themselves by fishing and gardening in small stone-walled plots. If you're searching for that bleak mystical Brittany ravaged by wind, sea and superstition then Sein may be able to help you. There are two hotels, and tourist information is provided by the town hall (tel: 02 98 70 90 35). Boats leave from Audierne year-round and take

Island cottages

about an hour. In summer there are several sailings, in winter only one in the morning; contact the Compagnie Maritime Penn-ar-Bed *(see page 79)*.

The southern coast of Brittany is less harsh and its islands are of a correspondingly gentler disposition. **Les Iles de Glénan**, 18km (11 miles) due south of Concarneau, is an archipelago of tiny islands that encircle a tranquil, clear-blue sea fringed with sandy beaches. Some of its smaller islands are bird reserves but there are no permanent inhabitants. In summer there is a sailing and diving school in operation. Most tourist boats call at the northern isle of St Nicholas. The crossing takes about an hour from Bénodet (Apr–Sep), and from Loctudy, Beg-Meil, Concarneau and Quimper (Jul and Aug only). Vedettes de l'Odet use glass-bottomed boats (tel: 02 98 57 00 58; www.vedettes-odet.com). Les Vedettes Bigoudènes (tel: 02 98 66 23 46) offer high-speed catamaran services to the islands from the same ports.

The **Ile de Groix**, a 45-minute crossing from Lorient or Quibéron, is a large flat island with steep cliffs 8km (5 miles) long. Some 2,500 people live there, many relying on summer tourism. There are sandy beaches to the east, two hotels, an Eco-musée and bicycles for hire. It is possible to take a car there – for details of sailings call the Société Morbihannaise et Nantaise de Navigation (SMNN; tel: 02 97 35 02 00/0 820 056 000; www.smnn-navigation.fr), or the island's Tourist Office, tel: 02 97 86 53 08.

Brittany's largest island is also its most southerly, **Belle-Ile**; it covers some 84 sq km (32 sq miles) and has many attractions. Compared to the other Breton islands it has a rare scenic variety, with exposed highlands, sheltered valleys, rugged cliffs and golden beaches. Belle-Ile has a historical and cultural pedigree too – Alexander Dumas set part of *The Three Musketeers* on the island (echoing real events that took place), and the citadelle in its principal town, Le Palais, redesigned by Vauban in the 17th century, was once a prison whose guests included Karl Marx. Sarah Bernhardt also lived here in flamboyant style and Flaubert, Monet, Proust and Matisse all stayed on the island.

Today Belle-Ile lives by tourism. It's ideal for walking, cycling and exploring; there are several hotels and many campsites. SMNN *(see above)* ferries leave from Quiberon-Port Maria (year-round; 45 minutes) to le Palais (expect long delays driving along the peninsula at peak times) and from Lorient to Sauzon (Apr–Sep; 25 minutes). You must reserve in advance if you wish to take your car. Compagnie Navix (tel: 02 97 46 60 00; www.navix.fr) sails from Vannes and Port Navalo (Apr–Oct) and La Trinité-sur-Mer (Jul–Aug). For tourist information on the island, tel: 02 97 31 81 93.

Plage Bonaparte

10. Beaches

A round-up of Brittany's best beaches.

Brittany has some of the best beaches in France. They seem to get bigger and better the more you travel around the region: even at the height of summer, when those in the most popular resorts are as packed with bodies as is decently possible, there is still enough sand to go round. They have variety too, and can cater for all our seaside fantasies – six-course family picnics, intrepid shrimp-hunting expeditions, existential movies starring lone man and a dog. Furthermore, unlike the beaches of the Mediterranean, they do not fail us if the sun disappears: out comes *la batte de cricket* and the boule, the kites, sand buggies and horses.

These beaches do have their drawbacks, though. One is that if the tide is out the mud is in, and it can be a long walk to find the sea. Seaweed can sometimes make the rocks slippery and walking treacherous. Sea temperatures rise to only 16–17°C (61–62°F) even at the end of August, but if you don't mind a bracing dip, you can still swim in September in clear blue water beside beautiful, almost deserted beaches along the south coast.

The best beaches are to be found along the northern and southern coasts. One indication of their merit is the award of a Blue Flag from the Foundation for Environmental Education in Europe. This indicates that a beach has attained the European Union's minimum standards for bathing water.

Blue Flag, sign of clean beaches

Golden sands on the Côte d'Emeraude

North Coast

Here a bunting of classic seaside resorts strings along the coast, all of which owe their long-standing popularity to the quality of their beaches. On the Côte d'Emeraude, Dinard is the most elegant of them all, its beach at St Enogat both chic and cheerful. There are also good family beaches backed up by busy resorts at St Cast-le-Guildo, St Jacut-de-la-Mer and St Quay-Portrieux.

On the Côte de Granit Rose the sinuous resort of Perros-Guirec has an extremely popular beach at Trestraou and a quieter one at Trestrignel. That of nearby Trégastel is famous for the anthropomorphic shapes of its pink granite rocks and there are other fine beaches at Trévou-Tréguignec and Trébeurden.

For wide expanses of sand with adequate but less overwhelming facilities try (going west) the beaches at Lancieux, Sables d'Or-les-Pins, Erquy, Le Val-André, Binic, Étables-sur-Mer, and, on the other side of the Côte de Granit Rose, the superb stretch at St Michel-en-Grève. For small out-of-town beaches where you must

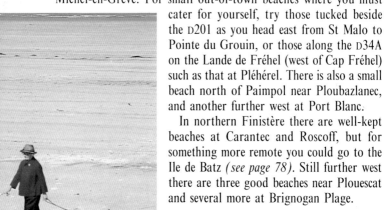

cater for yourself, try those tucked beside the D201 as you head east from St Malo to Pointe du Grouin, or those along the D34A on the Lande de Fréhel (west of Cap Fréhel) such as that at Pléhérel. There is also a small beach north of Paimpol near Ploubazlanec, and another further west at Port Blanc.

In northern Finistère there are well-kept beaches at Carantec and Roscoff, but for something more remote you could go to the Ile de Batz *(see page 78)*. Still further west there are three good beaches near Plouescat and several more at Brignogan Plage.

West Coast

Here the Breton coast turns wild. The shoreline is generally rocky and exposed with waters that are too dangerous for swimming. Nevertheless, sheltered sandy beaches can be found, such as the long curl of sand beside Morgat. There are also acceptable beaches at Plougastel-Daoulas, Camaret, Douarnenez (Les Sables Blancs most notably) and in the nearby resort of Tréboul.

Dogs: banned from beaches in summer

South Coast

Bénodet has one of the best beaches in Cornouaille and a great number of visitors to prove it. You may prefer the dunes and coves around Beg-Meil or visit the beaches near Fouesnant and La Forêt-Fouesnant. East from Lorient there is a long stretch of beaches as you head down towards the Presqu'île de Quiberon (the best at Etel and Erdeven). Quiberon can boast some of the nicest beaches along the south coast but they are often packed and access to them impossible on summer weekends. Carnac-Plage nearby is a better bet, or Locmariaquer further east; those in the know take the boat across to Belle-Ile where there are good beaches around Bangor.

One of Cap Fréhel's uncrowded beaches

As well as a seaboard stretching for some 1,207km (750 miles) Brittany also has 650km (403 miles) of navigable rivers and canals. Taking to the boats is a great way to enjoy the outdoors – leaflets advertising boat trips are available in travel agents and tourist offices; most of the excursions below run from April to October.

Sea Trips

If you like a voyage with an objective then you should take a day trip to one of the wild or gentle islands lying off the Breton mainland – *see pages 76–80*. There are also plenty of opportunities to cruise along the coast. From the Cale de la Bourse in **St Malo** or the Port de Plaisance in **Dinard** Emeraude Lines (tel: 02 23 180 180;

Taking to the boats

www.emeraudelines.com) operate trips to Les Iles Chausey (1hr 45mins one-way), the Ile de Cézembre (20mins), Cap Fréhel (2hrs 30mins) and around the Baie de St Malo (1hr). For a quick breath of sea air you can take their frequent ferry crossing from St Malo to Dinard (10 minutes). If you feel like going further afield, both Emeraude and Condor (tel: 02 99 200 300; www.condorferries. co.uk) offer day trips to the Channel Islands.

You can take a guided tour, by foot or on a little train, of the Baie du Mont St Michel with the Maison de la Baie (tel: 02 99 48 84 38), and learn about the bay's ecosystem: its wildlife and mussel beds, plus the high tides and shifting sands that make unguided tours inadvisable. The Association Bisquine Cancalaise run trips in an authentic replica of a *bisquine,* a local three-masted fishing boat; details available from their office on the quay at Cancale, tel: 02 99 89 77 87. All these trips can be booked in the travel agents next to St Malo's Tourist Office in the Esplanade St Vincent (tel: 02 99 56 64 48).

Birdwatchers should consider the three-hour round trip from **Perros-Guirec**, Ploumanac'h or Trégastel to the seabird sanctuary at Les Sept Iles, which is home to 27 species of nesting birds. Tel: 02 96 91 10 00 for information and reservations. Les Vedettes de Bréhat run full-day sea cruises departing from **Erquy**, **Le Val-André**, **Port Dahouët**, **Binic** and **St Quay-Portrieux** that call in at the Ile de Bréhat; reservations through the tourist offices in those ports.

Vedettes Bréhat sea cruises

From the port at **Morgat** on the Crozon peninsula Vedettes Rosmeur (tel: 02 98 27 10 71) run 45-minute trips out to the sea-caves and grottoes of the nearby cliffs as well as to the Cap de la Chèvre (2hrs) in July and August; they also run trips around the Baie de Douarnenez (1hr 15mins) from **Douarnenez** Apr–Sep.

From **Vannes** numerous companies offer trips around the Golfe de Morbihan, a 119 sq-km (46 sq-mile) inland sea peppered with 42 small islands. Information is available from the Tourist Office on rue Thiers (tel: 02 97 47 24 34) or from the kiosk at the Gare Maritime. Two of the largest islands, the Ile d'Arz and the Ile aux Moines are served by frequent ferries from Conleau (just south of Vannes) and Port Blanc (southwest of Vannes off the D101) respectively. A more luxurious way to travel is to take one of the pleasure cruisers operated by Navix (tel: 02 97 46 60 00) which embark from the Gare Maritime 1.6km (1 mile) south of Vannes towards Conleau. Their boats circulate between these two islands and Locmariaquer, Port Navalo, Le Bono and Auray and La Trinité-sur-Mer. Vedettes Angélus operate similar trips from the Port du Guilvin in Locmariaquer (tel: 02 97 57 30 29).

Another interesting excursion in the Golfe du Morbihan is to take a boat from Larmor-Baden across to the island of Gavrinis where there is a tumulus with extraordinary linear carvings on its granite slabs. These trips are organised by Vedettes Blanches Armor, tel: 02 97 57 15 27, and sometimes stop off at the Ile aux Moines.

River Trips

The tides determine the pace of trips up the **Rance** to Dinan. These are operated from St Malo and Dinard by Emeraude Lines *(see page 84),* with trips upriver normally taking around 2hrs 30mins with a bus connection back later (45mins).

Vedettes de l'Odet run round trips up the wooded banks of the

Placid waterways

Odet, 'France's loveliest river', to Quimper from Bénodet (2hrs 30mins) and Loctudy (3hrs 30mins); lunch or dinner is available on some sailings. With frequent trips in July and August between Quimper and Bénodet, you have the chance to spend most of the day in one of these resorts.

For reservations in Bénodet, tel: 02 98 57 00 58; Loctudy, tel: 02 98 87 45 63. Vedettes Glénan also run half-day trips from Concarneau up the Odet (tel: 02 98 97 10 31) in July and August.

Canal Trips

You could once sail right across Brittany via the Nantes-Brest canal, an ambitious project initiated by Napoleon in 1810. The canal was completed 26 years later and principally used to transport coal and slate – a business killed stone dead by World War I. The canal never recovered from the war and the construction of a dam at Lac de Guerlédan in 1928 severed the link decisively. Now it is only possible to travel between Pontivy and Port de Carhaix by canoe.

Today the region's canals are rarely used by commercial traffic and pleasure boats have the run of these placid waterways. A speed

limit of only 6kph (3.7mph) guarantees that any trip will be a leisurely progress through parts of Brittany few people see. Most boats and barges are hired well in advance by several holidaymakers for a week or fortnight but some companies will rent just for a day or weekend and some have boats that sleep

Mooring up at Dinan

only 2–4 persons. Bicycles can often be hired at the same time and a deposit is normally required.

Get in touch with a company directly and as early as possible – your chances of finding what you want will increase considerably if you avoid the peak months (August especially), but remember that many sections of canal close for works between mid-October and March. For more information contact either the Tourist Office in Redon (tel: 02 99 71 06 04, fax: 02 99 71 01 59) or the Brittany canal cruises website: Comité des Canaux Bretons Voies Navigables de l'Ouest, 6 rue de Lourmel, BP 182, 56308 Pontivy, tel: 02 97 25 38 24, fax: 02 97 07 00 00, www.bretagne-fluviale.net.

There are four main sections of canal that you can navigate – all part of a larger network of inland waterways. In Finistère this is along the River Aulne from Châteaulin to Port de Carhaix. Châteauneuf-du-Faou is the main centre for hiring boats; contact Aulne Loisirs Plaisance, Penn ar Pont, BP 76, 29520 Châteauneuf-du-Faou, www.aulne-loisirs.com.

In Morbihan a canal runs along the River Blavet connecting Hennebont to Pontivy. This links Lorient to the Nantes-Brest Canal, which runs from Pontivy to Redon to Nantes. Boats and barges can be hired from Comptoir Nautique de Redon, 2 Quai Surcouf, 35606 Redon, tel: 02 99 71 46 03, and Bretagne Plaisance, 12 Quai Jean-Bart, 35600 Redon, tel: 02 99 72 15 80, binfo@bretagne-plaisance.fr.

Another canalised section, the Canal d'Ile-et-Rance, runs between Dinan and Rennes, connecting with a navigable stretch running south along the River Vilaine to Redon. Boats and barges can be hired from Bretagne Croisières, tel: 02 99 71 08 05, fax: 02 99 72 42 45, http://members.aol.com.

Nantes-Brest canal

12. Walks

Walking is the best way to discover Brittany. During your visit, take yourself off down one of the many well-signposted coastal tracks, forest trails and canal-side towpaths. As Brittany has no mountains to speak of, few of these routes are arduous. You can find suggestions for walks at www.brittanytourism.com, and in Judy Smith's book entitled 'Holiday Walks in Brittany'.

Long-Distance Paths

France is criss-crossed by a network of long-distance trails known as *Sentiers de Grandes Randonnée*s (GR) These are well marked with red and white dashes and you could easily join one for a short walk or a day's hike. In Brittany more than 20 GRs pass through, most of them following east–west inland routes. In the north GR34 runs from Fougères to Morlaix, in central Brittany GR37 weaves from Montfort to Douarnenez via Josselin and Huelgoat, and in the south GR38 runs from Redon to Douarnenez via Châteauneuf-du-Faou and Quimper. GR380 tours the Montagnes d'Arrée and the parish *closes* and GR341 connects Paimpol and Pontivy. GRs are well mapped in the Topo-guides that detail their routes – in Brittany these are sold in local bookshops or they can be ordered from the Fédération

Française de la Randonnée Pédestre, Centre d'Information, 14 rue Riquet, 75019 Paris, tel: 01 44 899393, www.ffrp.asso.fr. Their other useful publications include Topo-Guides de Promenade et Randonnées, which set out circular walks and highlight points of interest along the way, and walking guides for families.

Coastal Paths

Some of the GR routes touch the Breton coast, most notably the GR34 that follows the sea all the way from Mont St Michel to Morlaix. You could spend a pleasant day walking from St Malo to Cancale via Rothéneuf following this route, or take in a portion of the 90-km (55-mile) section that runs from St Brieuc to Lannion and covers the Côte de Granit Rose. Some walks follow the old coastguards' footpaths *(Sentiers de Douaniers)* that skirt the cliffs and coves, for example the well-trodden path that runs from the oyster-beds of Cancale out to the Pointe de Grouin; the 'Watchpath Walk' from Le Val-André to Port Dahouët; the *sentier* from Perros-Guirec to Ploumanach; and the coastguard path that runs the length of Belle-Ile's Côte Sauvage.

Sentier de Pays

Feeding into these long-distance and coastguards' paths are numerous *Sentiers de Pays* (country trails), often radiating from inland hiking centres like Huelgoat and Paimpont. They offer good and easy walking through delightful countryside. Circular routes are often more convenient for a day's walking, and routes of varying length are described in guides to local *Petites Randonnées* (PR), which are available from bookstores and tourist centres. Some longer routes are known as *Grandes Randonnées de Pays* and marked with yellow and red dashes, like that in the Pays Gallo to the west of Dinan.

Long-distance trail

Country trail

Towpath Walks

If you like an easy level walk you might care to take in some of the 1,500km (900 miles) of towpaths *(chemins de halage)* that accompany Brittany's extensive network of inland waterways. GR37 follows part of the Nantes-Brest canal and is probably the most useful route. Further information is available from the Tourist Office, place de la République, 35600 Redon, tel: 02 99 71 06 05, fax: 02 99 71 01 59.

Huelgoat and the Parc Régional d'Armorique (Itinerary 3)

Tucked into the southeastern corner of the Monts d'Arrée, Huelgoat is a lakeside resort well placed both for easy walks in the surrounding forests and valleys and for hikes around the 172,000-ha (425,000-acre) Parc Régional d'Armorique. In Huelgoat look for the Café du Chaos at the eastern end of the lake where a path leads you down into the valley of the River Argent. Here enormous rocks carpeted with moss have created a series of sylvan grottoes – further east there are wooded walks out to Camp d'Artus, once an important Roman fort, or you can follow a canal, built in the 18th century to serve nearby lead and silver mines, round towards Le Gouffre. Further details from the Tourist Office in Huelgoat, tel: 02 98 99 72 32; http://rando29.free.fr provide a list of walks in the Parc.

Huelgoat and its forests

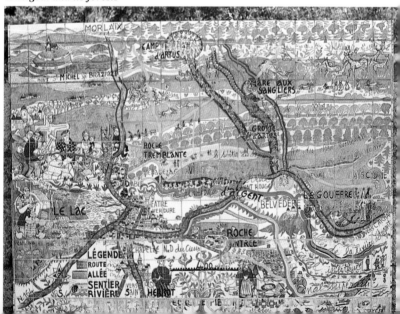

Valley of the River Argent

Mur-de-Bretagne and the Forêt de Quénécan (Itinerary 4)

Mur-de-Bretagne lies at the eastern end of the Forêt de Quénécan, close to the large, man-made Lac de Guerlédan and the Nantes–Brest canal. The area calls itself the *Coeur de Bretagne* (Heart of Brittany) and it's an excellent base for walking, camping, riding, boating, fishing and watersports. There are two very useful sources of information on what you can do here: the Pavillon du Tourisme in the centre of nearby Mûr-de-Bretagne and a smaller office located next to the 12th-century Abbaye de Bon Repos, just south of the N164 at the western end of the lake.

Well-marked trails

Walkers should consider following part of the GR341 path that skirts the shores of Lac de Guerlédan, or visiting the two smaller lakes, Lac de Fourneau and Lac des Salles. You can also buy booklets detailing *Petites Randonnées* in the area, or take a gentle stroll down the tree-lined towpaths running beside the canal – Gouarec is a good starting point for this. To the north of the N164 there is undulating heathland with steep gorges at Gorges du Daoulas (up the D44) and Gorges de Toul Goulic (both on the GR341), and further west at Gorges du Corong.

Paimpont and the Forêt de Brocéliande (Itinerary 5)

Paimpont stands at the centre of the Forêt de Brocéliande, a bewitching remnant of the dense primeval forests that once covered the Argoat. It's one of the many places King Arthur and his knights are believed to have visited in their search for the Holy Grail, and a legendary home of the sorcerer Merlin and the enchantress Viviane. Today Paimpont and its tangled forest is home to a thriving King Arthur industry that has many serious and bearded devotees, centered in the Château de Comper. Even if you have little time for such mysticism, the forest is at least a magical place to explore.

The Forêt covers some 7,000ha (17,300 acres), much of it still privately owned. Parts of it are far from ancient, being replanted with pines, but others are thick with mature beeches and oaks and a bright undergrowth of ferns *(fougères)*.

The Tourist Office in Paimpont (tel: 02 99 07 84 23) can provide you with information on walking the marked trails in the forest along with a map of the 'Circuit Brocéliande' that you can follow by car. You'll find it confusing and probably get lost, but then you are trying to discover the secrets of a spell-bound forest. Both the Château de Trécesson, where Merlin is said to be entombed in stone (not open to the public) and the Château de Comper, home of the Lady of the Lake, Viviane (park open to public) are easily found. So is the church at Tréhorenteuc, where some post-war wall-paintings achieve a rare marriage of Arthurian and Christian iconography. Not far from the church you can take a signposted walk to the steep-sided Val-sans-Retour and a rock where the fairy Morgane seduces unfaithful lovers.

You will also probably want to find Brocéliande's own Holy Grail, the elusive Fontaine de Barenton, whose waters are said to have therapeutic powers. This is the magic spring where Merlin is said to have first met Viviane. To get there take the D141 north from Tréhorenteuc, turning right at an unmarked hamlet known, significantly, as Folle-Pensée – if you reach La Saudrais you've gone too far. Pass through the hamlet following the signs to Camping Barenton, looking for a clearing and car park to the left signposted Fontaine de Barenton. From here you walk deep into the woods following the white dots painted on the trees. At a dot-less crossroads of forest tracks continue straight on up the hill – eventually the track divides three ways, at which point you turn left. Unfortunately all the signs in Brocéliande tend to get moved and defaced – perhaps by Merlin but much more likely by the anti-social hippies living in its woods.

Château de Trécesson

Moules à la marinière

Regional Specialities

Brittany's menus rightly give pride of place to the superb fish and seafood harvested from the waters off its long coastline. Expensive luxuries elsewhere, you'll find that lobsters and oysters here are all affordable, fresh and served without fuss. Lobster *(homard)* cooked *à l'Armoricaine* is often fêted as the region's premier speciality; the name, derived from the ancient Celtic word Armor, land of the sea, is often confused with the term *à l'Américaine* though the result is the same – a sauce based on tomatoes, onions, herbs, wine and brandy. A simpler way to eat lobster is to just have it *grillé* (grilled).

Oysters *(huîtres)* are another famous Breton delicacy and Cancale is the place to eat them – *see page 49*. Then there are clams *(palourdes, or praires* if they're small) and mussels *(moules, also farmed on the north coast) which come either *à la marinière* (cooked in white wine with shallots) or *farcies* (stuffed). *Langoustes* are smaller, clawless members of the lobster family sometimes known as spiny lobsters or seawater crayfish – not to be confused with *langoustines,* which are large prawns (similar to Dublin Bay prawns) of which scampi is one type. There are also freshwater crayfish *(écrevisses),* shrimps *(crevettes),* scallops *(coquilles Saint-Jacques)* and crabs – either the common *torteaux* or the flavoursome *araignées* (spider crabs). If you're feeling confused, the best thing to do is to order

a *plateau de fruits de mer* (platter of seafood) soon after you arrive in Brittany and decide what you like. You might be provided with a bib to avoid getting covered in juice as you extract strange creatures from their shells.

Brittany's fish are more straightforward: large quantities of cod *(cabillaud),* tuna *(thon)* and sardines are landed at its main ports while sole, plaice *(carrelet)* and turbot are often in the *poissonneries.* Monkfish *(lotte,* sometimes

Lobster traps

Typical pâtisserie

cooked in cider), sea bass *(loup de mer),* grey mullet *(mulet),* skate *(raie)* and eel *(anguille)* often feature on menus. *Soupe des poissons* is rarely disappointing while *cotriade,* a fish stew with onions, potatoes and herbs, is a Breton equivalent of *bouillabaisse.*

You'll probably find *à la bretonne* appears at least once on your menu: strictly speaking this is a garnish or sauce based on haricot beans, often served with lamb. Fish and eggs, however, can be served *à la bretonne* too, and usually this refers to *sauce bretonne,* a cream-and-white-wine sauce with leeks. *Potée bretonne* is like a hot-pot, often made with lamb, sausage and vegetables. Dishes (scallops and white fish in particular) also come *à la nantaise* or with *beurre blanc,* terms which refer to a white wine sauce enriched by butter that is supposedly the creation of Nantes chefs.

For meat, try some *gigôt* (leg) or *épaule* (shoulder) of *agneau pré-salé* (lamb from the salt-meadows of Mont St Michel – grazed on pastures washed daily by the sea); the lamb has a delicious ready-salted flavour; it is also expensive.

Brittany is also a good excuse to treat yourself to some *chateaubriand,* named after the St Malo-born author to whom this thick fillet steak (originally cooked with white wine, shallots and tarragon) was dedicated by the chef Montmireil. You could also try *canard nantais* – duck from Nantes – while *dinde* (turkey) and *pintade* (guinea fowl) are often good value.

95

Vegetarians are unlikely to be impressed by Breton cuisine. Vast tracts of Brittany may well be covered with vegetables but they never seem to make much of an appearance on the dining table; those that do – beans, cauliflowers, leeks, onions and artichokes in particular – are usually delicious. Salads are nearly always available.

Desserts are not especially Breton, though you may see strawberries billed 'from Plougastel'. The cheese basket will require a little research too – should you ask for *fromage breton*, you'll probably be given something similar to Port Salut made by the nuns of Campenéac or some *fromage du Curé* (also called *nantais* and not unlike St Paulin or Pont l'Evêque) invented by a priest of the Vendée in the 19th century.

If you're having lunch you might prefer to skip the dessert and call in later at a *pâtisserie* to investigate the sugary world of Breton cakes. *Far breton* is a custardy pudding filled with prunes or raisins – it tastes better than it sounds but it's not as irresistible as *kouign amann*, a treacly puff pastry made with extravagant amounts of butter. *Gâteau breton* is a catch-all term for what is sometimes a straightforward fruit cake, at others something similar to British lardy cake.

Breton baker's shop

Brittany is also famous for its *galettes* and *crêpes*, a fast food that dates back to neolithic times. For a quick snack these sweet or savoury pancakes are unbeatable – you can either buy them hot off a pavement *galettière* or sit down in a *crêperie* with a bottle of *cidre* and have an inexpensive, truly Breton meal. In Brittany *galettes* are normally savoury pancakes made with buckwheat flour *(sarrasin* or *blé noir)* and filled with anything from ham and eggs to shrimps and mussels. These are then followed by *crêpes*, sweet pancakes filled with combinations of jams, syrups and ice cream. *Crêpes dentelles* are 'lace' pancakes that originate from Quimper. They are like sweet rolled-up biscuits, crispy and thin: sometimes they're served with a dessert but you can also buy them in bakers and delicatessens. The term *galette* is also used to describe small shortbread biscuits made with butter – a Breton speciality that you can buy loose in *pâtisseries* or in pretty tins in gift shops.

Crêperie

Eating Out

Breakfast *(petit déjeuner)* is rarely included in the price of a hotel room and you shouldn't feel obliged to eat it there in the morning. It's quite acceptable (and often a lot cheaper) to wander off to a *boulangerie,* buy yourself a *pain au chocolat* or some *croissants aux amandes,* then go to a café to eat them.

For lunch, restaurants start filling up soon after noon and if you're not sitting down at a table by 2pm you could be in trouble. Lunch is still the main meal of the day for most Bretons, a leisurely affair that doesn't necessarily mean the consumption of vast amounts of food or wine.

In Brittany virtually all the restaurants offer two or three *menus à prix fixe* allowing you to select a choice of dishes for a fixed price. These are usually very good value, but don't include the price of drinks. You can also eat *à la carte,* generally more expensive and not always available late at night or at weekends. Eating out in France remains relatively inexpensive, despite the imposition of a 20.6 percent tax on restaurants and bars. Always investigate the *plat du jour,* as this is normally made from whatever's fresh and in season and may well be a Breton speciality.

For dinner, restaurants open around 7pm and most people will be tucking in by 9pm. If you're out in the sticks don't leave it too late – if you spot somewhere you like the look of earlier in the day don't hesitate to reserve a table, particularly if it's for Sunday lunch. Restaurants close at least one day a week *(ferme-ture hebdomadaire),* sometimes

Chouchen (mead), as drunk by Celtic deities

on Sunday evenings, sometimes Mondays. If you're heading for somewhere special be sure to ring first and watch out too for the annual *congé* (holiday), particularly if you're visiting in September.

Choosing a restaurant in Brittany shouldn't be difficult. In this part of France hotels often provide the best fare around and you may well find your most memorable meal comes not in a Michelin-fêted restaurant but at an unassuming two-star *Logis*. Recommendations for eating out have been included in the itineraries sections of this guide, but if you like to digest a detailed review of a restaurant before you eat in it consult one of the many guide books written by the self-appointed restaurant buffs and assessors of French cuisine who regularly gorge their way across Brittany.

Simple food, but good

The Muscadet vineyards around Nantes may no longer be officially a part of Brittany but most Bretons continue to regard the wines they produce as a quintessential feature of the region's gastronomic pleasures.

A crisp dry white wine with a high acidity, Muscadet is an ideal companion for the excellent seafood and fish caught off the Breton coast. One of the best-known Muscadets is from Sèvre-et-Maine; the expression *sur-lie* you often see on the label means that the wine has been matured on its lees (pips, skins) before being bottled, giving it a fruitier tang. Gros Plant, also from the Pays Nantais, is a less expensive, slightly coarser dry white.

Cider is the other principal Breton drink: that made from the apple trees around Fouesnant is probably the best, though in northern Brittany you're more likely to be served the equally palatable cider from the Rance valley. It is considered the natural complement to *crêpes* but many Bretons drink it without food. Most *crêperies* will bring you the sparkling and corked *cidre bouché* but if you go to a *cidrerie* (cider house) you may well be served their local cider – take care, it's often very strong.

Beer is widely available – if you want draught ask for *un demi* (a small one) or *une bière à la pression*; for bottled *une bière en bouteille*. Cervoise, the mystical brew of the Celts and strictly speaking a barley beer, can be tracked down in trendy bars and delicatessens: it's dark

Breton liqueurs

and powerful and wisely comes both capped and corked.

Brittany, or rather the Rennes-based Jacques Fisselier label, also produces a range of regional liqueurs. None should sway you from wrapping up your meal with a *calvados* (apple brandy) from next-door Normandy, but you may like to experiment with some of the miniatures sold everywhere. These include liqueurs made from peaches *(pêche blanche)*, blackberries *(mûre sauvage)* and Plougastel strawberries *(fraise)*. There's also a cider-based *eau-de-vie*, a *whisky de Bretagne* and BZH, a Campari-like apéritif. More widely made is *chouchen* or *hydromel*, a mead born of fermented honey and water which tends to smell of honey rather than taste of it.

For coffee a small black one is simply *un café*, a large black *un grand café*, a small white *un petit crème* and a large white *un café au lait* or *un grand café crème*. Cheers is *Santé!*

Shopping

Shopping in Brittany is easy, enjoyable and inexpensive. One joy is discovering the pleasures of the region's specialities, another is visiting those traditional French establishments – the time-absorbing *caves,* the mouthwatering *charcuteries* and *pâtisseries* – that draw so many of us to France.

Shops in Brittany tend to open between 9 and 10am and then close again between noon and 1pm for a lunch break of at least two hours. They open again between 2 and 3pm, although in the country areas you'll find this can stretch towards 4pm. They then stay open till at least 6pm and often 7pm. Even large supermarkets shut for lunch, and are closed by 7pm and on Sunday, so bear this in mind when planning your food shopping. However, in the resorts many will open longer hours during the summer season and in the cities some department and fashion stores stay open through the lunch hour. The majority of shops are closed on Sundays and Mondays, though some re-open on Monday afternoons.

Food shops such as *boulangeries* and *charcuteries* keep slightly different hours. These tend to open very early but take a longer lunch break, and there are usually one or two open on Sunday and Monday mornings. If you are planning a picnic be sure to buy everything before noon.

Herbal remedies

Fish shop

Local Specialities

Honey, *pré-salé* lamb from the salt marshes of Mont St Michel, Breton cheeses, cider from the Rance valley or Fouesnant and Breton liqueurs are all good buys. Look out for tins of Breton fish soup and seafood *pâtés* – the 'La Belle-Iloise' brand is made in Quiberon. Jars of home-made fish soup can also be bought in *poissonneries*.

At the *boulangerie* look for *far breton, kouign amann, galettes* and *crêpes dentelles*.

A rewarding purchase is a *crêpe*-making pan *(crêpière)* and all the necessary tools such as a rake *(râteau; rozell* in Breton) and a flat knife *(spatule; spanel* in Breton). Tell the sales assistant whether you will be using a gas or electric cooker and don't forget to buy some cider bowls and a jug to go with it. For clothes, Breton fishermen's sweaters, stripey matelot shirts and fishermens' caps are on sale everywhere. White duffle coats and wet weather sailing gear are good quality if you have need of them.

If you're heading for home, beer, wine, coffee and cheese are noticeably cheaper in France. You can sometimes make savings on kitchenware too, such as Le Creuset pans and knives. Tins of buttery *galettes* and packets of ready-made *crêpes* make nice gifts to take home.

Breton artichokes

Floral faïence

Handicrafts

Faïence is a distinctive hand-painted pottery that has been produced in Quimper for over three centuries. Designs follow classical lines and often include blue and yellow borders with a decoration of flowers or animals. Plates and bowls are the most common purchases but mugs, cups and saucers and other crockery are available.

You'll find the widest selection in Quimper, but *faïence* is sold throughout the region. There are also mass-produced imitations (the design is not fired into the pottery but painted on later) which are quite pleasant, considerably cheaper but not the real McCoy.

There is also a modern *faïence* produced by the Kéraluc factory with designs inspired by Brittany's Celtic heritage, as is the silver jewellery made by Toul Hoat. Wicker baskets are often sold in markets while *broderie bretonne* (Breton embroidery) and lace is sold wherever large numbers of tourists gather.

For other local handicrafts, craft fairs have the most original items – wood and granite are the favoured materials of local artists – and there is also a Breton Crafts Museum near Brasparts.

Markets

Markets are one of the delights of France and no less so in Brittany. At the seaside they blush bright with seafood stalls run by ruddy-faced fisherwomen; inland you'll find the whole town turns out on *jour de marché* for a chinwag amongst the cheese and chainsaw stalls; fresh food

Breton lacework

is brought to market by the producers themselves, organically grown vegetables are increasingly available, and nearly every market has a stall selling delicious savoury Vietnamese snacks.

Most markets are on only for the mornings, though in the larger cities like Quimper and Vannes some stallholders linger on well into the afternoon. In city centres like St Malo *intra-muros* or Vannes they can be split into different buildings a short walk from each other that will only sell, for example, fish, meat or flowers.

In the country markets they are often a jumble of stalls run by itinerant traders, an incongruous mix of live chickens and carving knives, berets and underwear. If you don't set out to buy anything you'll undoubtedly find something of interest – keep an eye out for stalls selling local honey, *chouchen* (mead), cheese, wicker baskets and perhaps even some Breton music CDs.

You may also encounter more specialist markets, perhaps selling livestock, crafts or *brocante* (antiques and second-hand goods). Fish auctions *(criées)* are a lively spectacle too: Concarneau's is the most famous and there are others of note in the ports at Roscoff, Audierne, Douarnenez and the southern ports of the Penmarch peninsula such as St Guenolé, Guilvinec, Lesconil and Loctudy.

Plenty of souvenirs

This is a guide to market days in the summer months.

Monday: Auray (fortnightly), Bénodet, Combourg, Concarneau, Douarnenez, Hédé, Ploërmel, Pontivy, St Quay-Portrieux, Trégastel, Vitré.

Tuesday: Étables-sur-Mer, Locmariaquer, Locronan (first in month only), Loctudy, Paimpol, Pont-Aven, St Malo, St Pol-de-Léon, St Servan, Trébeurden, La Trinité, Le Val-André.

Wednesday: Carnac, Paramé, St. Brieuc, Tréguier, Vannes.

Thursday: Carantec, Châteaulin, Dinan, Hennebont, Huelgoat (fortnightly), Lamballe, Lannion, Morlaix, Pont l'Abbé.

Friday: Auray, Concarneau, Douarnenez, La Trinité, Perros-Guirec, Quimperlé, St Brieuc, St Servan, St Malo, St Quay-Portrieux,

Saturday: Baud, Carhaix-Plouguer, Dol-de-Bretagne, Douarnenez, Guingamp, Josselin, Landernau, Paramé, St Brieuc, Vannes.

Sunday: Cancale, Carnac, Quimperlé.

Customs Allowances

For EU residents there are no restrictions on the movement of duty-paid goods carried by travellers between member states for their 'own personal use'; if you are carrying large quantities of alcohol or tobacco you may be required to prove that you are not intending to sell them. The guideline quantities for 'own personal use' are:

Alcohol: 10 litres spirits and 20 litres fortified wines and 90 litres wine (not more than 60 litres sparkling) and 110 litres beer.

Tobacco: 800 cigarettes and 400 cigarillos and 200 cigars and 1kg pipe or hand-rolling tobacco.

Allowances applying to travellers to/from non-EU countries:

Alcohol: 1 litre spirits or strong liqueurs over 22 percent volume or 2 litres fortified/sparkling wine, plus 2 litres still table wine.

Tobacco: 200 cigarettes or 100 cigarillos or 50 cigars or 250gms tobacco.

Châteaux, Gardens and Museums

Here are some attractions that are not included in the itineraries sections but which could easily be incorporated into your travels.

Near St Malo:

ROTHÉNEUF: **Manoir de Limoeleu**. 15th-century home of Jacques Cartier. Jul–Aug daily, Sep–Jun Mon–Fri.

BÉCHEREL (south of Dinan): **Château de Caradeuc**, the 'Versailles of Brittany', with magnificent classical park and views of the Rance valley. Park open daily 25 Mar–15 Sep, 16 Sep–31 Oct pm only, rest of year Sat and Sun pm only.

COMBOURG: **Château de Combourg**, turreted castle and park, birthplace of Chateaubriand and the setting for his bizarre *Mémoires d'Outre tombe*. Apr–Oct daily except Sat. Château open 2–5.30pm, park 9am–noon and 2–5.30pm.

PLEUGUENEUC (southeast of Dinan): **Château de la Bourbonsais**, 16th-century château with gardens, kennels and zoo. Open daily Apr–Sep 10am–7pm, Oct–Mar 2–6pm.

Breton château

Museum of Fishing, Concarneau

Near Roscoff:

Sᴛ Vᴏᴜɢᴀʏ (near Plouzévédé): **Château de Kerjean**, Renaissance château with collection of Breton furniture. Open Jun–Sep daily except Tues 10am–6pm; Apr–May daily except Tues 2–6pm; Oct–Mar Wed and Sun 2–5pm.

Parc Régional d'Armorique:

For general information on the park, tel: 02 98 81 90 08.

Méɴᴇᴢ-Mᴇᴜʀ, Hanvec: woodland estate with information about the Parc's work, plus enclosures of local wild and farm animals (popular with children) and the **Maison du Cheval Breton**. Open Jun–Sep daily 10am–7pm; May 1.30–5.30pm, closed Sat; rest of the year Wed and Sun only 10am–noon and 1–6pm; closed Jan.

Mᴏᴜʟɪɴs ᴅᴇ Kᴇʀᴏᴜᴀᴛ (near Commana): restored **watermills** and tannery – part of the Ecomusée des Monts d'Arrée. Open Jul–Aug daily 11am–7pm; Jun daily 10am–6pm; rest of year Mon–Fri 10am–6pm, Sun 2–6pm.

Mᴀɪsᴏɴ Cᴏʀɴᴇᴄ (near St Rivoal): restored **17th-century debt-collector's house**, part of the Ecomusée des Monts d'Arrée. Open daily Jul–Aug 11am–7pm, June 2–6pm.

Mᴏᴜʟɪɴ Vᴇʀɢʀᴀᴏɴ, Sizun: **Maison de la Rivière** offers an opportunity to learn about the wildlife of the river, and gives details of nature walks in the area. Open Jul–Aug daily 10am–6.30pm; Jun and Sep Mon–Fri 10am–noon and 2–5pm, Sun 2–5pm; Oct–May Mon–Fri 10am–noon and 2–5pm.

Sᴛ Hᴇʀɴᴏᴛ, south of Crozon: **Maison des Minéraux** has 500 mineral specimens illustrating the geology of this part of the Massif Armoricaine. Open daily Jul–Sep 10am–7pm; Jun 10.30am–12.30pm and 2–7pm; Oct–May daily except Sat 10am–noon and 2–5.30pm.

Tʀᴇɢᴀʀᴠᴀɴ (near Plomodiern): **Musée de l'Ecole Rurale** housed in restored early 20th-century school. Open Jul–Aug daily 10.30am–7pm; May, Jun, Sep daily 2–6pm; Apr, Oct–Nov daily except Sat 2–5pm; Dec–Mar Mon–Fri 2–5pm.

Sᴄʀɪɢɴᴀᴄ: **Musée de la Faune Sauvage et de la Chasse**; 70 species of small animals. Open Jun–Sep 10am–noon and 2–6pm, closed Tues.

Lᴏǫᴜᴇꜰꜰʀᴇᴛ: **Maison des Pilhaouerien**, devoted to the rag-and-bone men of the Monts d'Arrée. Open Jul–Aug 10am–noon and 2–6pm, rest of year groups by appointment; tel: 02 98 99 62 36.

Mᴏɴᴛ Sᴛ Mɪᴄʜᴇʟ ᴅᴇ Bʀᴀsᴘᴀʀᴛs (near Brasparts): **Maison des Artisans**, craft museum on the highest point of the Monts d'Arrées. Open daily Apr–Aug 11am–7pm, Sep–Mar Sat–Sun 11am–7pm.

Near Quimper:

St Goazec (near Châteauneuf-du-Faou): **Domaine de Trévarez**, late 19th-century château set in 85 ha (210 acres) of woods and gardens. Open Apr, May, Jun and Sep daily 1–6pm; Jul–Aug daily 11am–6.30pm; Oct–Mar Wed, Sat, Sun 2–5.30pm.

Combrit (near Bénodet): **Musée de Musique Mécanique**, idiosyncratic museum of mechanical musical instruments collected by a local enthusiast. Open May to September 2–7pm.

Pont l'Abbé: **Musée Bigouden**, traditional Breton costumes. Open Apr–May, Oct Mon–Sat 10am–noon and 2–5pm; Jun–Sep daily 10am–12.30pm and 2–6pm.

Douarnenez: **Musée du Bateau**, historic boats and fishing with working boatyard. Open Apr–Oct Mon–Sat 10am–12.30pm and 2–6pm; Jun–Sept daily 10am–7pm.

Near Vannes:

St Marcel: **Musée de la Résistance Bretonne**, dedicated to the local Resistance. Open 15 Jun–15 Sep daily 10am–7pm; rest of year daily 10am–noon and 2–6pm; closed Tues 16 Sep–1 Apr.

Sarzeau: **Château de Suscinio**, 13th-century castle. Small **museum of Breton history**. Open daily Apr–May 10am–noon and 2–7pm; Jun–Sep 10am–7pm. Rest of year at odd times.

Thalassotherapy

The medicinal value of sea air, seawater and seaweed has long been known to the Bretons. Brittany has 11 thalassotherapy centres offering revitalising tonics, underwater massage in jet-pools, skin cleansing with seaweed mud-packs, etc. Plan to stay for at least a weekend. Book ahead and take relevant medical records. Useful websites include: www.thalasso-france.com; www.tourismebretagne.com; www.thalgo.co.uk.

St Malo: Les Thermes Marins, Grande Plage du Sillon, 35401 St Malo, tel: 02 99 40 75 75, fax: 02 99 40 76 00, www.thalasso-saintmalo.com.

Dinard: Novotel Thalassa, Avenue du Château Hébert, 35802 Dinard, tel: 02 99 82 78 10, fax: 02 99 82 78 29.

Perros-Guirec: Centre de Thalassothérapie de Perros-Guirec, boulevard Thalasso, 22700 Perros Guirec, tel: 02 96 23 28 97, fax: 02 96 91 20 75.

Roscoff: Clinique de Ker Léna, 2 rue Victor Hugo, 29650 Roscoff, tel: 02 98 24 33 33, fax: 02 98 24 32 34. Institut de Thalassothérapie Roc-Kroum, BP 28, 29681 Roscoff Cedex, tel: 02 98 29 20 00, fax: 02 98 61 22 73.

DOUARNENEZ: Thalas Santé, Treboul, 29175 Douarnenez, tel: 02 98 74 47 47, fax: 02 98 74 45 24.

BÉNODET: Maison de Santé Médicale, 299950 Bénodet, tel: 02 98 - 66 26 26.

QUIBERON: Institut de Thalassothérapie de Quiberon, Pointe du Gourlvars, 56170 Quiberon, tel: 02 97 50 20 00, fax: 02 97 30 47 63.

BELLE ILE: Institut de Thalassothérapie Goulphar, 56360 Le Palais, Belle-Ile-en-Mer, tel: 02 97 31 80 15, fax: 02 97 31 51 69.

CARNAC: Centre de Thalassothérapie, Avenue de l'Atlantique, 56343 Carnac, tel: 02 97 52 53 54, www.thalasso-carnac.com

VANNES: Institut de Thalassothérapie Louison Bobet, Port Crouesty, 56640 Arzon, tel: 02 97 53 90 90, fax: 02 97 53 74 26.

Nightlife

Brittany is not a place for night owls – come 10pm in a small country town you could find the place deserted. Most visitors are content to round off their day's sightseeing with a leisurely dinner followed by a digestif in a local café. That said, the seaside resorts provide their visitors with evening entertainment in summer. Casinos lead the way, the most popular are in St Malo (Esplanade St Vincent) and Dinard (Palais d'Émeraude); you will need to take your passport. All the resorts have at least one disco. In less seasonally minded cities such as Quimper or Vannes, you'll find bars and cafés with live music.

Sport

Visitors to Brittany can pursue many of the genteel and some of the more insane sports that man has devised. If you have a particular interest, the quickest way to find out what facilities are available is to call into the local tourist office. For spectators there is also a busy calendar of tournaments, regattas and competitions throughout the year. The following list is a brief guide to sports that make the most of the region's outstanding natural features. The Brittany tourist board (www.region-bretagne.com) can provide information and brochures on golf, horse-riding, fishing, walking, waterways, sailing and cycling.

Breton Sports

Your best chance to catch these are at one of the many Celtic-flavoured festivals that take place in the larger towns or cities – the Festival Interceltique held in Lorient every August is the biggest. They will often include a sports day featuring demonstrations or competitions

'Breton wrestling' (1895), by Paul Sérusier

– Breton wrestling *(Ar Gouren)* is the most popular, followed by numerous trials of strength such as tossing the caber, tug-of-war, discus throwing and *tire-bâton,* where the contestants try to lift each other using a pole. The atmosphere is similar to the Highland Games in Scotland.

Windsurfing and Water-skiing

Windsurfing is the favourite watersport in Brittany, with big Atlantic rollers attracting the experts and sheltered coves offering good nursery conditions for beginners. The best beaches for windsurfing are those between Audierne and Concarneau but boards *(planches à voile)* and tuition are available from surfing centres all around the coast. The Pointe de la Torche, near Pont l'Abbé, is where the serious aquabats head for.

Water-skiing is available in many resorts – for a detailed list of facilities contact the Ligue de Bretagne de Ski Nautique, BP 99, 49303 Cholet. Diving off the Breton coast offers remarkable opportunities like exploring the Er Lannic Cromlech in the Gulf of Morbihan. The waters around Brittany's offshore islands are particuarly clear, and there is plenty of marine life to see. Log on to www.subchandlers.com for a list of diving clubs in Brittany.

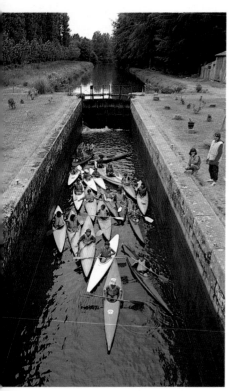

Canoeing, the Nantes–Brest canal

Sailing

The challenges and pleasures of yachting off the Breton coast draw thousands of sailors here each summer. A list of harbour facilities and yachting schools is available from the Comité Régional du Tourisme in Rennes, tel: 02 99 28 44 30. In most resorts pleasure craft can be hired.

Sand yachts or buggies *(char à voile)* are a dry alternative well suited to Brittany's long hard sand beaches – for details contact the Ecole Nationale de Voile at St Pierre-Quiberon, tel: 02 97 30 30 30.

Canoeing

Intrepid canoeists who care to try sea kayaking should contact the Comité Régional de Bretagne de Canoë-Kayak, www.crbck. dhs.org. For the more gentle sport of river and canal canoeing, contact the local tourist office *(see page 124 for addresses)*.

Cycling

The French adore cycling and Brittany is no exception. Every Sunday its roads are illuminated by the bright jerseys of the cycling clubs out for a day's ride. If you want to join in, each *département* has a local Comité Départemental de Cyclotourisme which you can contact through its head Tourist Office *(see page 124)*. Most towns have cycle shops that hire out bikes (a large deposit is usually required).

Horse Riding

This is a rewarding way to get deep inside Brittany's countryside. Horses can be hired from many *centres équestres*, either by the hour or as part of an organised cross-country hack. Contact the Association de Tourisme Equestre en Bretagne, tel: 02 98 91 02 02.

Angling

Sea fishing trips are available in some resorts, such as those from St Malo arranged by Emeraude Lines *(see page 84)*, and you will usually find quaysides punctuated by boards advertising such trips. Fishing

Sea fishing

from the shore or a harbour wall can be rewarding with the right equipment, and you are free to join the Bretons who paddle at low tide searching for shrimps and crabs.

For river fishing it is necessary to join a local club (Association de Pêche et de Pisciculture) to get a licence – the local tourist office or the staff of the local fishing tackle shop will usually help you in this matter. The banks of the River Aulne around Châteaulin are popular for trout and salmon fishing.

Golf

Reflecting the popularity of golf in Brittany, the region has 32 golf courses affiliated to the Ligue de Golf de Bretagne (3 Allée René Hirel, 35000 Rennes, tel: 02 99 31 68 80, fax: 02 99 31 68 83). Most are on the coast with year-round facilities and 18 holes. Within reach of St Malo you'll find courses at Dinard (tel: 02 99 88 32 07), Sables d'Or-les-Pins (tel: 02 96 41 42 57), Le Tronchet (tel: 02 99 58 96 69) and Dol-de-Bretagne (tel: 02 99 73 54 44).

Further west you'll find Golf des Ajoncs d'Or at St Quay-Portrieux (tel: 96 71 90 74) and Golf de St Samson at Pleumeur Bodou (tel: 02 96 23 87 34).

In Finistère there is the Golf de Brest-Iroise Landerneau (tel: 02 98 85 16 17) and one further south within range of Quimper at La Forêt Fouesnant (tel: 02 98 56 97 09).

There are also courses in Morbihan near Auray (9 holes; tel: 02 97 56 85 18), at Baden (tel: 02 97 57 18 96), St Gildas-du-Rhuys (tel: 02 97 45 30 09) and on Belle-Ile (tel: 02 97 31 64 65).

Near Rennes there is the 9-hole Golf de Cesson-Sévigné (tel: 02 99 83 26 74) and the 18-hole Golf de la Freslonnière (tel: 02 99 14 84 09).

Calendar of Special Events

In Brittany, the year's celebrations are marked by two quite different occasions: the serious acts of religious devotion known as *pardons* and the cultural fêtes inspired by the region's Celtic and Breton heritage. Sometimes the two meet – a *pardon* may well culminate in a fair with folk dancing and stalls selling *crêpes* and local specialities while a *fête* will often begin its festivities with a religious ceremony, like the blessing of the fishing nets that opens the Fête des Filets Bleu in Concarneau.

Pardons derive their name from the Catholic church's tradition of granting indulgences to their parishioners on Saint's Days in order that their sins might be pardoned. The ceremonies often include the taking of vows and the seeking of cures. Many of their rites have been observed annually since the 16th century, even earlier in some cases, and *pardons* have therefore preserved many features of Breton culture that might otherwise have died out. For this reason they are considered to be part of Brittany's tourist appeal, though if you are not a religious person you may feel your presence is intrusive.

Some *pardons,* like those at Ste Anne d'Auray, Ste Anne-la-Palud and Le Folgoët, attract thousands of pilgrims; others are smaller and may include the blessing of specific subjects such as lawyers, cattle, apple trees or even cars. Ceremonies generally commence with Mass and proceed to open-air services outside the church. The high point is a pious procession, sometimes candlelit, in which the devout, dressed in local costume and singing Breton hymns, walk through the fields and streets carrying banners, statues and relics.

Festive Dinan

In the evening there is confession and vespers, after which the lay festivities commence.

Regular *pardon*-attenders say that the atmosphere and solemnity of these occasions vary from place to place and year to year. If you manage to catch one, you should see women wearing *coiffes* (lace head-dresses), hear the Breton language and perhaps feel the force of the superstitious winds that have buffeted Brittany over the centuries.

If, however, all you want to see is some traditional Breton dress and folk dancing, to hear the sound of the *biniou* (bagpipe) and the *bombarde* (oboe), to drink cider and eat *crêpes* as you watch some Breton wrestling, then you may find Brittany's secular festivals more rewarding. Their objectives are simpler: to keep Breton folklore alive, foster the cultural links between the seven Celtic regions – Brittany, Ireland, Scotland, Wales, Cornwall, the Isle of Man and Galicia in Spain – and have a damn good time. Information and an annual programme is available from tourist information centres *(see page 124)* or the Institut Culturel de Bretagne, 1 rue Raoul-Ponchon, 35069 Rennes, tel: 02 99 87 58 00, fax: 02 99 87 58 08.

The following calendar is only a guide and you should check with the local tourist office before setting out. On public holidays *(jours fériés)* some museums and tourist sights are open, but most businesses, shops, and all banks are closed.

January / February

The French celebrate everything with a grand meal and the New Year is no exception. Fireworks and *crise de foie* (crisis of the liver) caused by generous alcohol consumption follow. The **1st** is a public holiday.

March/April

Pâques is a serious religious celebration in Brittany and **Easter Sunday** and **Monday** are public holidays. **1 April** is known as Poisson d'Avril, the equivalent of April Fool's Day.

Breton coiffé

May

The **1st**, Fête du Travail (Labour Day), is suitably marked by a day off work. The **8th** is a public holiday too, VE Day. **Ascension** (usually mid-May) is a public holiday and also the day of St Herbot's *pardon*. On the **second Sunday** there is a *pardon* at Quintin (near St Brieuc) and on the **third Sunday** one in Tréguier to honour St Yves, patron saint of lawyers. During May St Brieuc hosts a festival of Breton folklore, Le Mai Breton, with a *pardon* on the last weekend.

June

The Sunday and Monday of **La Pentecôte** (Whitsun) are public holidays (usually late May/early June). There is also a *pardon* at Moncontour (near Lamballe) and a Fête de Toulfouen (birds) at Quimperlé. The **following Sunday** there is a *pardon* at Rumengol, a traditional place of pilgrimage in the midst of the Forêt de Cranou. On the **23rd**, Midsummer's Eve, there is a *pardon* at St Jean du Doigt (near Morlaix) in which the village's prize relic, the index finger of St John the Baptist (brought here in 1437) is dipped in a basin to produce holy water. On the **last Sunday** there is a *pardon* at Le Faouet (near Quimperlé) while Carhaix-Plouguer honours its famous son, the warrior-linguist La Tour d'Auvergne.

July

Either at the end of June or early in July, the capital, Rennes, kicks off a heavy month of celebration with its ten-day Festival des Tombées de la Nuit, a celebration of Breton culture. On the coast St Brieuc hosts a festival of Breton music in early July. St Malo also stages a folkloric festival, Le Clos Poulet, in July and from mid-July to mid-August its annual Festival du Musique Sacrée.

On the **first Sunday** there is a major *pardon* at Guingamp and on the **second Sunday** a Fête des Brodeuses (embroidery) in Pont l'Abbé and a folkloric festival Ajoncs d'Or (golden gorse) in Lamballe. That day also marks Locronan's Troménie (also called the Fête des Collines Bleues), a pilgrimage in

honour of St Ronan that follows the route to his hermitage; every sixth year there is a Grand Troménie. The **14th**, Bastille Day, is an explosive public holiday marked by firework displays. Mid-July also finds Paimpol celebrating its fishing links with Newfoundland and Iceland with a Fêtes des Terre-Nuevas.

On the **third Sunday** Fouesnant, set deep in the cider country south of Concarneau, holds its Fête des Pommiers (apple trees). In Douarnenez there is a Fête des Mouettes (seagulls). On the **25th** and **26th** one of the region's most famous *pardons* takes place, the Pardon

Breton festivities, 1863

of Ste Anne d'Auray (near Auray), mother of the Virgin Mary and patron saint of Brittany.

The week before the **last Sunday** in July Quimper holds its highly recommended Fêtes du Cornouaille, a week of Breton celebrations that attracts performers from all the Celtic nations. On that Sunday there is a *pardon* on the Ile de Batz while that at Le Folgoët (north of Landerneau) in honour of St Christopher includes the blessing of motor cars. There is also a *pardon* in St Quay-Portrieux at the end of July.

August

On the **first Sunday** in Pont-Aven there is a Fête des Fleurs d'Ajoncs d'Or (golden gorse), started in 1905 by the poet Théodore Botrel who also wrote the well-known song 'La Paimpolaise'.

There is also a *pardon* in Huelgoat on the same day.

During the first fortnight of August an International Celtic Arts festival is held in Lorient, a lively cultural jamboree with stalls, shows and live music. In mid-August there are also Festivals of Breton Dance in Guingamp (La St Loup) and Châteauneuf-du-Faou and a *pardon* and Fête de la Mer in St Cast-le-Guildo (west of Dinard).

On the **second Sunday** St Briac-sur-Mer holds its Fête des Mouettes (seagulls) with Breton dancing, processions and nocturnal celebrations known as Fest-Noz. There is also Breton dancing in Douarnenez, a Fête des Bruyères (heather) in Beuzec-Cap-Sizun (near the Pointe du Raz), a Festival de la Mer in Plougasnou (north of Morlaix) and a Festival Folklorique des Genets d'Or (golden broom) in Bannalec (north-west of Quimperlé).

Mid-August is when Perros-Guirec holds its Fête des Hortensias (hydrangeas) while on the south coast La Baule has a Grand *pardon* and a weekend of Journées Culturelles Bretonnes. The **15th** is the Assumption of the Virgin Mary and a public holiday. In Plomodiern (north of Locronan) there is a Festival Folklorique du Ménez-Hom, in Vannes the Grande Fête d'Arvor, in Port Manech (south of Pont-Aven) a Fête de l'Aven and in Audierne (near the Pointe du Raz) a Fête d'Armor. There are also *pardons* in Moncontour (near Lamballe), Pont-Croix (near Audierne), Plougastel-Doulas (east of Brest) and Perros-Guirec.

On the **third Sunday**, there is a *pardon* in pretty Rochefort-en-Terre (east of Vannes), while Carnac holds its Grande Fête des Menhirs and Concarneau its spectacular fishermen's festival, the Fête des Filets Bleus. On the **last Sunday** of the month there are *pardons* in Châteaunouf-du-Faou (south-west of Carhaix-Plouguer) and at the Chapel of Ste Anne-la-Palud (north-west of Locronan), one of the best-attended in the Breton calendar.

September

On the **first Sunday** the *pardon* for Our Lady at Le Folgoët (north of Landerneau) is one of the greatest in Brittany. The church at Le Folgoët (Fool's Wood), built after a miraculous lily bearing the words 'Ave Maria' was found flowering above a simpleton's grave, has been a place of pilgrimage since the 15th century. There is also a *pardon* at Camaret. On the **8th** at Josselin there is a *pardon* in honour of Notre Dame du Roncier, also known as the 'Barker's Pardon' after three local children were cured of epilepsy at a festival in 1728.

On the **second Sunday** Carnac holds a cattle festival in honour of St Cornély. On the **third Sunday** there are *pardons* at Belz (west of Auray), Plouha (south of Paimpol) and Pontivy. On the **last Sunday** there is a Fête des Voeux (vows) at Hennebont (near Lorient) and at Pont l'Abbé a *pardon*. At the end of September or early in October Dinan stages its Fête des Remparts, a weekend of medieval frolics. On the **29th** there is a Michaelmas fair at St Brieuc.

November

All Saints' Day (Toussaint), the **1st**, is a public holiday, as is the **11th**, Armistice Day.

December

On the **4th** there is a *pardon* at Le Faouet. Noël (Christmas) is a time for parties and cultural events and the **25th** is naturally celebrated with the grandest meal of the year.

Practical information

When to Visit

Brittany has a relatively short holiday season – providing you visit between April and October you can expect to find enough places open to keep yourself fed and entertained. Many attractions are closed until Easter (except during the February school holidays) and it's often a month or so before they're fully geared up for the peak period, July and August. This ends abruptly with *la rentrée* (the end of the school holidays), and by mid-September you'll find things starting to go quiet.

This scenario only applies to the seaside resorts and inland rural areas. In the cities and larger ports life rolls on, with the museums and tourist attractions shortening their opening hours in the winter months. If you intend to tour around, late spring and early autumn are a good bet as roads and hotels are far less crowded and there's a fairly good chance of fine weather. If you're staying put, July and August promise the warmest temperatures, but avoid travelling during the first, middle and last weekends of August, when the whole of France appears to be on the move and many roads are gridlocked.

If you want to attend a *pardon* or one of Brittany's lively cultural festivals, *see page 112.*

Climate

Brittany's weather is not unlike that of Britain's: unpredictable, yet sometimes glorious. Summers are good when they happen, similar to those in southwest England but tending to last longer. Sunshine cannot always be guaranteed but warm temperatures can – on average 21°C (70°F) in July and August. Winters are unlikely to be harsh, except on the west coast. It is often breezy, and the further south you travel, the better the weather generally is. Plan for rain and be pleasantly surprised.

Documents

All visitors require a valid passport. Visitors from non-EU countries (including Canada and the US) do not require a visa if staying under 3 months – more details can be obtained from your nearest French consulate.

Electricity

220 volts. Sockets generally take round two-pin plugs and most non-European appliances will need a transformer.

Time Difference

For most of the year France is one hour ahead of Greenwich Mean Time and 6 hours ahead of Eastern Standard Time.

Money Matters

Along with most of the EU, France adopted the Euro (€) in January 2002. Credit cards are widely accepted, including in petrol stations and supermarkets. The best exchange rates are given by banks displaying a *Change* sign. Avoid changing money at hotels, which often charge a high commission.

Don't Forget...

Film, map, sunglasses, swimming costume and books. French hotels are notoriously mean with their towels and soap, so take these along too.

HOW TO GET THERE

By Air

Flying to Brittany is ideal for business trips or for a short, impulsive break. If you plan to travel around try to arrange a fly/drive deal before you leave as car hire is expensive in France. There are a lot more flights in the summer months, with fewer connections available in winter.

KLM UK fly from London Stansted to Brest during the summer months; log on to www.klmuk.com for details.

Air France fly direct from London to Nantes and Rennes, tel: 0845 0854111; and from the US to Paris, tel: 212 830 4000/1 800 237 2747; www.airfrance.com.

British European Airways fly from London City Airport to Rennes and from Gatwick to Nantes. For details in the UK tel: 08705 676676, www. flybe.com. It is also possible to fly to Paris and take an internal flight to Brest, Quimper, Lorient, Rennes, or Nantes with Air France. Air France and SNCF (French Railways; www.sncf.fr) offer joint air/rail deals via Paris

By Sea

The main attraction of travelling to Brittany by sea is it allows you to take your own car – by far the easiest way to tour the region. Prices vary according to season and it is advisable to book well ahead if you plan to travel in the holiday periods. All the ferry companies offer inexpensive short-break fares.

Brittany Ferries sail from Portsmouth to St Malo (9hrs) and from Plymouth to Roscoff (6hrs). They also sail from Cork to Roscoff (14hrs). For details in the UK tel: 0870 5360 360; in Ireland, tel: 021 4277801; www. brittanyferries.com.

Condor Ferries sail from Poole and St Malo (4½hrs) from late May to end September. For reservations and information, tel: 0845 345 2000, www. condorferries.co.uk. Condor and **Emeraude Lines** also sail between St Malo and the Channel Islands. In St Malo, tel: 02 99 200 300 (Condor), and 02 23 180 180 (Emeraude).

Irish Ferries sail from Rosslare to Roscoff (tel: 1890 313131 from the Republic of Ireland; 0800 018 2211 from Northern Ireland; 561 563 2856 in the US; www.irishferries.ie) Another alternative is to take a ferry to Normandy

and drive across to Brittany. **Brittany Ferries** have crossings from Portsmouth to Caen and from Poole to Cherbourg. **P&O Portsmouth** sail from Portsmouth to Cherbourg and Le Havre, tel: 0870 242 4999, www.poportsmouth.com. **Irish Ferries** also sail from Rosslare to Cherbourg.

By Train

The Channel Tunnel enables passengers to travel by Eurostar from Britain to Brittany via Paris. High-speed (TGV) rail links make the journey from Paris to Rennes in only two hours, and to Brest in four hours. There are also fast rail connections from Paris to St Malo and along the south coast to Nantes and Quimper.

For fares and times on **Eurostar**, tel: 0990 186 186, www.eurostar.com. **Rail Europe** can reserve train tickets in France. Contact them at 178/9 Piccadilly, London W1, tel: 08705 848 848, www.raileurope.co.uk.

In the US, contact the French Government Tourist Office, tel: 212 838 8700, www.francetourism.com, or Rail Europe at www.raileurope.com/us. Brittany-bound trains leave from the Gare de Montparnasse – prior reservation is required to travel on TGVs.

By Road

Rennes is 352km (219 miles) from Paris, Quimper 570km (355 miles). An *autoroute* (toll motorway) runs from Paris to the edge of Brittany. From there fast, toll-free N roads run along its northern and southern coasts. There are also good N roads to Brittany from the Channel ports in Normandy. For information on travel through the Channel Tunnel with a car contact Eurotunnel, tel: 08705 353535, www. eurotunnel.com.

International coach operators offer cheap services from the UK to Brittany

via a cross-channel ferry to St Malo or Roscoff; details from Eurolines, tel: 01582 404511.

WHERE TO GO

If you want to see Brittany rather than France, go west. Basse Bretagne, an area traditionally seen as lying west of an imaginary line running south from

Old-fashioned farming methods

St Brieuc to Vannes, is where Breton culture is most evident. The north coast, particularly along the Côte d'Émeraude and the Côte de Granit Rose, has the best beaches – wide and sweeping sands with room for everyone. The south is gentler, with wooded river valleys and a softer, sunnier ambience. The west coast is the most dramatic, rising to cliffs and rocky headlands buffeted by angry seas. Inland you'll find rolling farmland patched with ancient woods and man-made lakes, gentle rivers and rigid canals. In Finistère the land rises to moorland and the protected open spaces of the Armorica National Park. Then there are the islands, some flat and severe, others mild and bucolic.

For a short city-based break consider

St Malo, Quimper or Vannes; for a *gîte*-based holiday pick an inland village within easy reach of the north coast beaches or one in the vicinity of the River Odet.

For a complete change consider the Ile d'Ouessant, for a complete rest Belle-Ile. Go to Carnac for mystery, the parish closes for history, Cancale for oysters and Quimper for pottery.

GETTING AROUND

The best way to see Brittany is by car and most people take their own vehicles over there by cross-channel ferry. Car hire is expensive in France but may be more practical for short trips. Public transport is efficient but not always convenient, as rail routes favour east–west journeys. Travelling by train and then hiring a bicycle at a local station is one possible solution. In such a relaxed landscape, cycling, walking, riding and river journeys are all viable alternatives.

Maps

Drivers should use Michelin route map No. 230 Bretagne or its smaller sections 58, 59 and 63, all 1:200,000. To make the most of the countryside, follow the picturesque routes marked in green. An alternative is the Red Series *carte touristique* 105 (1:250,000) published by the Institut Géographique National, the French equivalent of the UK Ordnance Survey. The Institut also publish a Green Series (1:100,000), which shows footpaths, and a more detailed Orange Series (1:50,000) and Blue Series (1:25,000).

By Car

Brittany has no toll roads but has good dual carriageways (N roads) for fast journeys. The region is also criss-crossed with quiet minor roads that are well worth exploring. Apart from peak times *(see page 116)*, the roads are generally uncongested, and a pleasure to drive on. Petrol is slightly cheaper than in the UK.

Drive on the right and take particular care at junctions. *Priorité à droite*, once a cause of confusion for visiting motorists, has been phased out, except in built-up areas, where you must give way to anyone coming from a side turning to the right. An orange diamond on the side of the road indicates that you have priority; the same sign with a black diagonal line through it means you don't. Signs reading *Cédez le passage* and *Vous n'avez pas la priorité* both require you to give way.

Seatbelts must be worn by front seat travellers, and motoring offences can attract stiff on-the-spot fines. Speed limits are 130kph (80mph) on motorways, 110kph (68mph) on dual carriageways, 90kph (56mph) on other roads and 60kph (37mph) in towns. Crash helmets must be worn by motor cyclists.

Driving

Drivers must be at least 18 years old and have a full driving licence (UK, US and Canadian licences are accepted). Fully comprehensive insurance is recommended. If you are taking your own car you must carry the vehicle registration document, insurance certificate and a letter of authorisation from the owner if it is not registered in your name. A green card, available from your insurance broker, is an internationally recognised document proving that you have minimum insurance cover; it does not provide any extra cover. It is not compulsory when driving in EU countries as long as you have your insurance certificate with you, but may prove useful in case of an accident.

It is advisable to carry a red warning triangle, obligatory if you do not have hazard warning lights. You will also need a complete kit of spare light bulbs, headlamp-converters for right-hand drive and a GB sticker. Unleaded petrol *(essence sans plomb)* is widely available.

Car Hire

Car hire is expensive in France and it is best to arrange it before you leave. Many airlines offer fly/drive deals and SNCF offer rail/drive packages.

By Taxi

Taxis can be hired in the cities and resorts from taxi ranks or called by telephone. If you are embarking on a long journey agree a price first.

By Bus and Coach

Bus services connect parts of Brittany not covered by the trains. Most are run by private companies and their timetables are designed to meet local needs rather than those of foreign travellers. SNCF also run useful bus services between their stations and nearby towns. Timetables are available from bus stations *(gares routières)* and tourist offices.

Coach excursions to many of Brittany's sights, including special trips to see *pardons,* can be booked through travel agents, such as **Tourisme Verney** in St Malo (16 rue Auguste Fresnel, tel: 02 99 82 26 26) and **Voyages Castric** in Combrit (1 rue Général de Gaulle, tel: 02 98 51 96 23), as well as at some SNCF stations.

By Train

Brittany's railway provides good east-west connections with routes from Rennes along the northern coast to Brest and along the southern to Quimper. North-south travel is trickier but a link line connects these two termini and there is a service between St Malo and Rennes. There are also lines from Guingamp to Carhaix and St Brieuc to Loudéac with SNCF buses continuing south.

Train services are efficient and bicycles can be hired from many stations. If you will be travelling a lot by train, consider getting a rail pass, which allows discounted travel in France for a fixed period. Discounts are also available for travellers under 26, families and senior citizens. Further information on these options is available from Rail Europe, 178/9 Piccadilly, London W1, tel: 08705 848 848, www.raileurope. co.uk. In the US, log on to raileurope.com/us.

By Bicycle

Cycling is a good way to see Brittany. With a network of minor roads, cyclist-friendly motorists and a good supply of repair shops, you can't go wrong.

Bikes are carried free on cross-channel ferries and for a small fee on trains and buses. Bikes can also be hired by the day from most SNCF stations. Information on routes is available from the Cyclists Touring Club, Cotterell House, 68 Meadrow, Godalming, Surrey GU7 3HS, tel: 01483 417217, www. ctc.org.uk.

By Horse

Riding across Brittany is an attractive proposition. The region has a good stock of equestrian centres, some of its *gîtes d'etape* offer stabling, and there are plenty of circuits and itineraries to follow. Hiring a *roulotte* (horse-drawn caravan) is another possibility. For further details contact the Centre Equestre du Guilou near Brest, tel: 02 98 89 50 68, fax: 02 98 89 90 18. The tourist board's website, www.brittanytourism. com lists a range of riding holidays.

By Boat

Brittany's canals provide a leisurely way to see the region – *see pages 84–7.*

By Foot

'Walking is virtue, tourism deadly sin' as Bruce Chatwin put it. *See pages 88–92.*

WHERE TO STAY

Always book well ahead. This is absolutely essential if you plan to visit Brittany in July or August. If you are touring it is well worth ringing a hotel in the morning to make a reservation for that night – they will normally expect you to arrive by 6pm. Should you find everywhere full, the tourist offices are usually very helpful.

Hotels

Hotels in France are graded from one- to four-star with prices quoted per room. The majority of those available in Brittany are two-star with a room for two with bath costing around €38 per night. Breakfast is extra. Standards vary but soft mattresses and orange wallpaper on the ceiling are a consistent feature. Some hotels have good restaurants but lousy rooms, others vice-versa. If you plan to do a lot of hotel-hopping you may find it useful to buy a specialist hotel guide – *see page 128.* A listing of all Brittany's hotels and their facilities is available from the French Government Tourist Office *(see page 124)* or www. hotels-de-bretagne.com.

It is quite normal to be shown a room and then asked if it is suitable: if it isn't don't hesitate to ask for another, perhaps for a room with a view *(une chambre avec vue)* or one away from the noise on the street *(loin des bruits de la rue).* If you are only staying one night some hotels may ask you to agree to eat in their restaurant before they will grant you a room.

Logis de France, an association of family-run hotels with a distinctive

green and yellow logo, are invariably good value with pleasant rooms and friendly staff. There are over 300 *logis* and *auberges* in Brittany and a brochure is available from Logis de France, 83 avenue de l'Italie, 75013 Paris, tel: 01 45 84 84 84, fax: 01 45 83 59 66, www.logis-de-france.fr. For something more luxurious try the **Relais et Châteaux** group (tel: 00 800 2000 00 02 in France, or 1 800 735 2478 in the US; www.relaischateaux.fr); for something quiet try **Relais du Silence**, 17 rue d'Ouessant, F-75015 Paris, tel: 01 44 49 79 00, fax: 01 44 49 79 01, www.silencehotel.com).

Some hotels in Brittany can be booked through travel agents in the UK; these will also have details of the numerous companies offering short-break packages there, such as **Direct Travel**, tel: 0870 7700370.

The following hotels are all good value: **Auberge St Thégonnec**, 6 place de la Marie, 29410 St Thégonnec, tel: 02 98 79 61 18. **Hôtel du Prieuré**, Locronan, tel: 02 98 91 70 89. **Le Relais Brocéliande**, 35380 Paimpont, tel: 02 99 07 84 94.

Other Accommodation

Chambres d'Hôtes are similar to Britain's bed-and-breakfast accommodation, but better. Prices are comparable to a two-star hotel but include breakfast. They tend to be in rural areas or on the outskirts of town and are a good way to meet Bretons. You can normally have an evening meal as well, which you may eat with the rest of the family. You'll see signs advertising Chambres d'Hôtes on the roadside, and local tourist offices can provide lists in their area. **Fermes-Auberges** offer a similar arrangement but are on working farms. You can also B&B in a Breton *château* or manor; contact B&B France (tel: 01491-578803; www.bedbreak.com), or French Country Guesthouses (www.bedbreakfast-france.com).

Gîtes offer self-catering accommodation in holiday cottages and apartments for a week or more, mostly in inland rural areas. They often get booked up months in advance. For a handbook and details contact Brittany Ferries *(see page 117)*.

Gîtes are also advertised in the Sunday papers, while travel agents have details of the many companies offering all-inclusive self-catering holidays in Brittany. **Gîtes d'Étape** are basic, dormitory-style local authority-owned hostels situated near walking, riding and cycling routes. They are open to all, unlike **Auberges de Jeunesse**, youth hostels, which are open only to members

of the Youth Hostel Association; details from YHA, Trevelyan House, Dimple Road, Matlock, DE4 3YH, tel: 01629 592702, www.yha.org.uk; the French Youth Hostel Federation's website is www.fuaj.org/eng. There are no age restrictions for French youth hostels.

Camping

Brittany is ideal for camping and has more sites than any other region of France. Most are near the coast and some are extremely sophisticated, more like canvas hotels where campers book in for a week or two's holiday. They are graded from one- to four-star and can get booked up during high season. For details contact Camping Plus Bretagne, tel: 02 98 87 87 86, fax: 02 98 82 21 19, www.campingplus.com/en.

There are also municipal sites, those on farms *(camping à la ferme)* and those called *aire naturelle de camping*, which have much more basic facilities.

USEFUL INFORMATION

Tourist Offices

Tourist offices are an invaluable source of information. In France they are known as Syndicats d'Initiative or Offices du Tourisme, and you will find them in most towns. They are normally open 10am–noon and 2–6pm.

In the UK contact the French Government Tourist Office, 178 Piccadilly, London WIV 0AL, tel: 0906 8244123, www.franceguide.com. In the US, tel: 212 838 8700, www.francetourism.com. In Brittany, the Comité Régional du Tourisme, 1 rue Raoul Ponchon, 35069 Rennes, tel: 02 99 28 44 30, www. brittanytourism.com, provides a wealth of information and ideas, and their website lists the contact details of every tourist office in Brittany. Each *département* also has its own head office, or Comité Départemental du Tourisme:

Côtes d'Armor: 29 rue des Promenades, BP 4620, 22046 Saint-Brieuc, tel: 02 96 62 72 00, www.cotesdarmor.com.

Finistère: 11 rue Théodore-Le-Hars, BP 1419, 29104 Quimper, tel: 02 98 76 20 70, www.finisteretourisme.com.
Ille-et-Villaine: 4 rue Jean Jaurès, BP 6046, 35060 Rennes, tel: 02 99 78 47 47, www.bretagne35.com.
Morbihan: Hôtel du Département, BP 4000, 56009 Vannes, tel: 02 97 54 06 56, www.morbihan.com.

are all positive attractions. Travel facilities are encouraging and some ferry companies offer free passage to the cars of registered disabled travellers. Most French railway stations have facilities for the disabled and local tourist offices will often provide free guides to the access, transport and accommodation available in their area.

There is also plenty of information available in the UK. The French Government Tourist Office *(see page 124)* can provide details of hotels that make provisions for disabled guests, and a leaflet with addresses of French disability organisations that can help. For information and support, consult the Royal Association for Disability and Rehabilitation, at 250 City Road, London EC1V 2AS, tel: 020 7250 3222, www.radar.org.uk. The charity Holiday Care provides an information pack on France, available from 2 Victoria Road, Horley, Surrey RH6 7TZ, tel: 01293 774535, www.holidaycare.org.uk. The online magazine www.disabilityview. co.uk provides suggestions for holidays in France.

Consulates

Ireland: 4 rue Rude, 75116 Paris, tel: 01 44 17 67 00. **UK**: 18bis rue d'Anjou 75009, tel: 01 44 51 31 00. **US**: 2 rue St Florentin, 75382 Paris, tel: 01 43 12 22 22; 30 quai Duguay-Trouin, 35000 Rennes, tel: 02 23 44 09 60.

Tipping and Service

Most restaurants include service in their bills *(service compris)* but satisfied diners will often leave a tip as well. In bars and cafés it is customary to leave the waiter a few coins, and a similar amount should be given to hotel porters and taxi drivers, though it's not obligatory. In bars you will normally pay a higher price for your drinks if you sit down at a table rather than stand at the bar.

Facilities for the Disabled

Brittany is a viable summer holiday destination for disabled travellers. The proximity of the region, its beaches and invigorating sea air, its ready access to modern medical facilities and the possibility of thalassotherapy treatments

Children

Brittany is ideal for children: it offers safe family holidays by the sea and a good range of exhausting amusements and diversions. Here children are not just tolerated, but welcomed as guests in bars and restaurants – as long as they are well behaved.

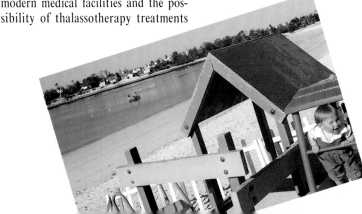

papers are sold in the larger resorts and towns, and it is often possible to pick up BBC radio broadcasts.

Telephone

The French telephone system works well. Most public telephone boxes now only take a phonecard *(télécarte)*, which can be bought from post offices, *tabacs* and newsagents. For long international calls you may find it easier to use one of the pay-at-the-end booths situated in or near main post offices. You can also telephone from bars and cafés but this may be more expensive, as it always is from hotels.

To call within Brittany and the rest of France, you must dial the full 10-digit number. To call Brittany from the UK dial 00 33 then the 10-figure number minus the initial zero.

An engaged tone sounds like a rapid beeping. The operator is 13, Directory Enquiries 12. Calls are 50 percent cheaper between the hours of 10.30pm and 8am weekdays and from 2pm on Saturday onwards at weekends.

Facilities for babies and children are good: nappies and powdered milk are widely available in supermarkets, most restaurants have high chairs and hotels can usually provide a cot *(lit bébé)* for a small supplement. In the main resorts there are children's clubs on the beaches in July and August. In restaurants children's portions can be ordered, or simply ask for another plate. But not all restaurants in Brittany are as welcoming (in some the poodles seem to get better treatment), so if your child has a tendency to run riot, pick your establishment with care.

It's against the law for children under 10 to travel in the front seat of a car. On ferries and trains children under four travel free.

To dial other countires first dial the international access code 00, wait for the second tone, then the country code: Australia (61); Germany (49); Netherlands (31); Spain (34); UK (44); US and Canada (1), then the number minus any initial zero. If using a US credit phone card, dial the company's access number: Sprint, tel: 0800 99 0087; AT&T, tel: 0800 99 0011; MCI, tel: 0800 99 0019.

The Internet

There is a huge amount of information on France and Brittany on the Internet;

MEDIA & COMMUNICATION

Regional papers are widely read in France and Brittany's local paper *Ouest-France* has the largest circulation in the country. Some English news-

most towns, hotels and tourist attractions have their own websites. As well as the websites mentioned elsewhere in this chapter, the following contain useful information:

www.brittany-guide.com
www.easy-breaksbrittany.com
www.region-bretagne.fr
www.bretagne.com

BUSINESS HOURS

Shops and Restaurants

Shops are generally open 9am–noon, 2–6.30 or 7.30pm, and closed on Sundays and Mondays. Food shops keep slightly longer hours – see *Shopping, page 100.* For restaurants see *Eating Out, page 97.*

Banks

Open 9am–noon, 2–4pm weekdays. You will need your passport when cashing traveller's cheques. ATMs that take credit and debit cards are widely available.

Post Offices

Known as PTT or *Poste* and open at least 9am–noon, 2–5pm weekdays, 9am–noon Saturday in main towns. Stamps *(timbres)* can also be bought in a tobacconists *(tabac)* and often wherever postcards are on sale.

HEALTH & EMERGENCIES

EU visitors are advised to take an E111 form with them to France, available from main post offices in the UK. This entitles you to medical and dental treatment from the French health service, though you will have to pay for this at the time of treatment and then claim a refund. This will normally cover at least 75 percent of treatment costs and 40 percent of prescription charges. Refunds are paid by the local sickness insurance offices, known as *Caisses Primaire d'Assurance-Maladie,* so be sure to get the address of your nearest office before you leave.

If you are treated by a doctor or dentist show them your form straightaway to ensure they are *conventionée* (members of the scheme) and make sure you get a *feuille de soins* (signed statement of treatment) before you leave the surgery. When you buy medicines at a pharmacist make sure the prescription is attached to the *feuille de soins* as well as the *vignettes* (stamps) on the medicine containers. Everything must

then be sent to the *Caisse* for a refund. If you are hospitalised they will normally do this on your behalf but check first.

Taking out private medical or travel insurance is recommended – it saves a lot of hassle, although it is still necessary to keep all receipts.

For minor ailments you can visit a *pharmacie,* which is a good source of advice and devoted solely to the dispensing of medication. They will also be able to tell you where the nearest doctor *(médecin)* or dentist is.

Emergencies

For the Police call 17, for an Ambulance 15, for the Fire Brigade 18. For medical emergencies in cities you can also call the Service d'Aide Medicale d'Urgence (SAMU) whose numbers are listed in the front of phone books.

Crime

Brittany is generally a safe and law-abiding region and if you take the common-sense precautions you normally would at home you should experience little trouble. As in all holiday resorts, however, petty theft from cars and so on can be a problem so be sure not to invite it. Good travel insurance offers some consolation for any losses incurred; before leaving home, be sure to read the small print to check the excess and maximum amount paid out for individual articles.

FURTHER READING

General

For background reading the *Insight Guide: Brittany* offers in-depth essays on the region including a detailed history and articles on the Bretons and their culture. Pierre-Jakez Hélias' *The Horse of Pride* (Yale University Press) is a moving autobiographical account of rural life in the pays Bigouden during the early 20th century. *La Routes des Peintres de Cornouaille*, available in French or English from tourist offices and bookshops, is an excellent, well illustrated guide to the region and the artists who worked there.

History

Aubrey Burl's *A Guide to the Stone Circles of Britain, Ireland and Brittany* attempts to throw light on the mysterious menhirs. Further historical insights are provided in *The Lost Love Letters of Heloise and Abelard* by Constant J.

Mews and Neville Chiavaroli, a translation and analysis of the correspondence between the famous 12th-century lovers. The *Selected Letters of Madame de Sévigné* (Penguin Classics) is a view of 17th-century Brittany seen from a château near Vitré, and the *Mémoires d'Outre-Tombe* of René Chateaubriand (in French only) is an entertaining chronicle of a late 18th-century childhood spent in a château at Combourg.

Fiction

For fiction, Honoré de Balzac's *The Chouans* (Penguin Classics) is an early romantic novel inspired by the Royalist uprising in Brittany that followed the French Revolution, while some of the action in Alexander Dumas' *The Three Musketeers* (Penguin Classics) takes place in Brittany.

The story of the Battle of the Thirty is retold in *Sir Nigel* by Sir Arthur Conan Doyle. Jean Genet's *Querelle of Brest* (Faber) is a lyrical low-life tale of a young sailor and the dubious characters he encounters, while Colette's *Ripening Seed* (Penguin), written in 1923, is a tender tale of an adolescent romance set near Cancale.

The Ebony Tower by John Fowles (Pan) is a collection of stories inspired by Arthurian and Breton myths, with the title novella set in Paimpont forest. *Legends and Romances of Brittany* by Lewis Spence recalls the days of knights in shining armour. Nevil Shute's *Most Secret* is a World War II thriller set in Brittany.

Hotels

For detailed recommendations of special places to stay, try Alastair Sawday's *French Hotels, Inns and Other Places*. Hotels that are out of the ordinary from a design or architectural point of view are decribed in Herbert Ypma's guide, *Hip Hotels: France*.

NOTES

ACKNOWLEDGMENTS

Additional photography
3, 21A, 25, 41, 62/63, 68, 81, 87,   **Brittany Ferries Photo Library**
93, 100, 105, 110, 113, 116, 119A, 123A, 126B

4/5   **D & J Heaton/Apa Photo Agency**
10, 11, 13, 36, 37B, 109, 114   **Editions Dufy**
8/9   **Tony McCann**
21B, 22, 23, 24, 26, 27, 28, 32B, 33, 42B, 43,   **Nigel Tisdall**
48, 50, 55B, 61, 62A, 65, 66B, 70, 75, 76,
77B, 78, 79, 80, 81, 82, 83, 85, 88, 89, 90, 91,
94, 96, 97, 98B, 112, 113A, 118, 119B, 120, 122,
123B, 124B, 125A, 127

Cover Design   **Tanvir Virdee**
Front cover   **Pictures Colour Library (Belle-Ile, Sauzon)**
Back cover   **Jeroen Snijders/APA**
Cartography   **Berndtson & Berndtson, Maria Randell**

Index

A

accommodation, 122
airlines, 117
Anne, Duchess of Brittany, 13, 18, 42, 73
angling, 111
antiques, 57, 65
aquariums, 62, 75
Argoat, 12
Armorican massif, 12
Artichoke War, 17, 19
Auray, river, 86

B

Barbe-Torte, Alain, 18
Barrage de la Rance, 20
Basilica St Saveur, Dinan, 54
beaches, 81–83
Beauport, Abbaye de, 26
Belle-Ile, 80
Bénodet, 34
Bernard, Émile, 36
bowling, 75
Brasparts, 31, 106
Brest, 32, 78
Breton food, 94–99
Breton language, 17
Breton liqueurs, 57
Buvette de la Plage, Le Pouldu, 38
business hours, 127

C

Camaret, 32
camping, 124
canal trips, 86
Cancale, 50
canoeing, 110
Cap Fréhel, 24
Carnac, 67
Cartier, Jacques, 18, 44, 46, 105
Celts, 12, 18
Chateaubriand, René de, 45
Château de Caradeuc, Bécherel, 105
Château de Combourg, 105
Château de Comper, Paimpont, 92
Château de la Bourbonsais,
    Pleugueneuc, 105
Château de Kerjean, St Vougay, 106
Château de Suscinio, Sarzeau, 107
Château de Trécesson, Paimpont, 92
Château de Trévarez, St Goazec, 107
cheeses, 96
children, 125
Chouans, 14–15, 19, 41
'chouchen', 75
cider, 99
climate, 116
'coiffes', 16
Combat des Trente, 18, 43
Concarneau, 35
consulates, 125

Cornouaille, 33
corsairs, 48
Côte Ajoncs, circuit de la, 28
Côte de Granit Rose, 27, 28
Côte d'Émeraude, 20, 82
craft fairs, 102
'crêpes', 96
Crozon Peninsula, 32
cycling, 110, 121

D, E

Dinan, 63
Dinard, 21, 82, 84
disabled travellers, 125
drinks, 99
driving, 121
Duguay-Trouin, René de, 46, 48
duty free, 104
Eco-museé d'Ouessant, 78
electricity, 117
emergencies, 127
Erquy, 82, 85

F

'faïence' (pottery), 66, 102
'far breton', 96
ferries, 117
'fêtes', 112
fish, 94
Fontaine de Barenton, Brocéliande, 92
Forêt de Brocéliande, 91
Forêt de Paimpont, 43
Forêt de Quénécan, 34, 91
Fort la Latte, 23
Fort National, St Malo, 46

G

'galettes', 96
gardens, 55, 62, 105
Gauguin, Paul, 16, 36–39
Gavrinis, 85
'gîtes', 123

golf, 111
gorges, 91
Guesclin, Bertrand du, 18, 53
Guimiliau, 59
Gulf of Morbihan, 75, 85

H

handicrafts, 102
health, 127
hiking, 89
horse-riding, 111, 122
hotels, 122
Huelgoat, 30, 90

I

Ile de Batz, 62, 78
Ile de Bréhat, 27, 76
Ile de Groix, 80
Ile de Sein, 79
Ile d'Ouessant, 78
Iles des Glénan, 80
Internet, 126
islands, 76

J, K

Jean V, Duke of Brittany, 13, 28
jewellery, 102
Josselin, 41
Kerguéhennec, 43
Kernascléden, 38
King Arthur, 12, 91
King Gradlon, 64
'kouign amann', 96

L

Lac du Guerlédan, 86, 91
lace, 102
Lampaul-Guimiliau, 60
Landes de Lanvaux, 42
Le Pouldu, 37
Le Val-André, 24, 82, 85

Locmariaquer, 69, 85
Locronan, 33

M

Maison Cornec, St Rivoal, 106
Maison de la Rivière, Sizun, 106
Maison des Artisans, Brasparts, 106
Maison des Minéraux, St Hernot, 106
Maison des Pilhaouerien, Loqueffret, 106
Maison du Cheval Breton,
    Ménez-Meur, 106
Maison Marie Henry, Le Pouldu, 37
Manoir de Limoeleu, Rothéneuf, 105
maps, 120
markets, 103
Ménez-Hom, 32
menhirs, 12, 67
Montagnes Noires, 12
Monts d'Arrée, 12, 31
Morgat, 83, 85
Moulin Vergraon, Sizun, 106
Moulins de Kerouat, Commana, 106
Mur-de-Bretagne, 39
Musée Bigouden, Pont-l'Abbé, 107
Musée d'Archéologie, Vannes, 75
Musée de la Faune Sauvage et
    de la Chasse, Scrignac, 106
Musée de Pêche, Concarneau, 35
Musée de la Résistance Bretonne, St
    Marcel, 107
Musée de l'Huître, Cancale, 52
Musée de Musique Mécanique,
    Combrit, 107
Musée de Pont-Aven, 37
Musée de Préhistoire, Carnac, 69
Musée des Beaux Arts, Quimper, 65
Musée des Beaux-Arts, Vannes, 75
Musée des Phares, Ouessant, 79
Musée du Bateau, Douarnenez, 107

N, O

Nantes-Brest Canal, 14, 86, 91
Napoleon, 14

nightlife, 108
Nominoë, Duke of Brittany, 13, 18
Notre Dame de Kroatz Batz, 62
Odet, river, 63, 85
oysters, 37, 49–52

P

Paimpol, 25
Paimpont, 44, 91
Parc Régional d'Armorique, 30, 90, 106
'pardons', 112
parish closes ('enclos paroissiaux'), 57
Perros-Guirec, 28, 82, 84
Ploërmel, 44
Pointe de Bilfot, 25
Pointe de l'Arcouest, 26, 77, 85
Pointe de Penhir, 32
Pointe des Espagnols, 32
Pointe du Grouin, 50
Pont-Aven, 35–38
Pors-Even, 26
Port Blanc, 25

Q, R

Quimper, 63, 85
railways, 121
Rance, river, 21, 53, 85
restaurants, 97
river trips, 85
Rochers Sculptés, Rothéneuf, 49
Roscoff, 61, 78, 105
Rothéneuf, 44, 49

S

Sables d'Or-les-Pins, 24, 82
sailing, 110
St Briac-sur-Mer, 22
St Cast-le Guildo, 82
St Corentin cathedral, Quimper, 64
St Cornély, 70
St Herbot, 31
St Jacut de-la-Mer, 82

St Malo, 22, 44, 84
St Michel-en-Grève, 29, 82
St Pierre cathedral, Vannes, 74
St Quay-Portrieux, 82, 85
St Servan, 47
St Thégonnec, 57
St Yves, 27
sand yachting, 109
sea trips, 84
seafood, 94
Sentiers de Grandes Randonnées, 88
Sentiers de Pays, 89
shopping, 101
sports, 109
Stamped Paper Revolt, 14
Surcouf, Robert, 46, 48

T

telephone, 126
thalassotherapy, 107

time difference, 117
Tour de Coëtquen, Dinan, 55
Tour Solidor, St Malo, 21, 47
tourist offices, 124
Tours d'Elven, 39
towpath walks, 90
Trébeurden, 82
Tréboul, 83
Trégastel, 25, 82
Tréquier, 27
Trieux, river, 85
Tumulus de St Michel, Carnac, 70

V, W

Vannes, 39, 71, 85
walks, 88
water-skiing, 109
wind-surfing, 109

INSIGHT
Pocket Guides

Insight Pocket Guides pioneered a new approach to guidebooks, introducing the concept of the authors as "local hosts" who would provide readers with personal recommendations, just as they would give honest advice to a friend who came to stay. They also included a full-size pull-out map. Now, to cope with the needs of the 21st century, new editions in this growing series are being given a new look to make them more practical to use, and restaurant and hotel listings have been greatly expanded.

Also from Insight Guides...

Insight Guides is the classic series, providing the complete picture with expert and informative text and stunning photography. Each book is an ideal travel planner, a reliable on-the-spot companion – and a superb visual souvenir of a trip. 193 titles.

Insight Maps are designed to complement the guidebooks. They provide full mapping of major destinations, and their laminated finish gives them ease of use and durability. 100 titles.

Insight Compact Guides are handy reference books, modestly priced yet comprehensive. The text, pictures and maps are all cross-referenced, making them ideal books to consult while seeing the sights. 127 titles.

INSIGHT POCKET GUIDE TITLES

Aegean Islands	Canton	Israel	Nepal	Sikkim
Algarve	Cape Town	Istanbul	New Delhi	Singapore
Alsace	Chiang Mai	Jakarta	New Orleans	Southeast England
Amsterdam	Chicago	Jamaica	New York City	Southern Spain
Athens	Corfu	Kathmandu Bikes	New Zealand	Sri Lanka
Atlanta	Corsica	& Hikes	Oslo and Bergen	Stockholm
Bahamas	Costa Blanca	Kenya	Paris	Switzerland
Baja Peninsula	Costa Brava	Kraków	Penang	Sydney
Bali	Costa del Sol	Kuala Lumpur	Perth	Tenerife
Bali Bird Walks	Costa Rica	Lisbon	Phuket	Thailand
Bangkok	Crete	Loire Valley	Prague	Tibet
Barbados	Croatia	London	Provence	Toronto
Barcelona	Denmark	Los Angeles	Puerto Rico	Tunisia
Bavaria	Dubai	Macau	Quebec	Turkish Coast
Beijing	Fiji Islands	Madrid	Rhodes	Tuscany
Berlin	Florence	Malacca	Rome	Venice
Bermuda	Florida	Maldives	Sabah	Vienna
Bhutan	Florida Keys	Mallorca	St. Petersburg	Vietnam
Boston	French Riviera	Malta	San Diego	Yogjakarta
Brisbane & the	(Côte d'Azur)	Manila	San Francisco	Yucatán Peninsula
Gold Coast	Gran Canaria	Melbourne	Sarawak	
British Columbia	Hawaii	Mexico City	Sardinia	
Brittany	Hong Kong	Miami	Scotland	
Brussels	Hungary	Montreal	Seville, Cordoba &	
Budapest	Ibiza	Morocco	Granada	
California,	Ireland	Moscow	Seychelles	
Northern	Ireland's Southwest	Munich	Sicily	